New Directions for Institutional Research

John F. Ryan
EDITOR-IN-CHIEF

Gloria Crisp
ASSOCIATE EDITOR

New Scholarship in Critical Quantitative Research—Part 2: New Populations, Approaches, and Challenges

Ryan S. Wells
Frances K. Stage

EDITORS

Number 163
Jossey-Bass
San Francisco

New Scholarship in Critical Quantitative Research—Part 2:
New Populations, Approaches, and Challenges
Ryan S. Wells, Frances K. Stage (eds.)
New Directions for Institutional Research, no. 163
John F. Ryan, Editor-in-Chief
Gloria Crisp, Associate Editor

NEW DIRECTIONS FOR INSTITUTIONAL RESEARCH (ISSN 0271-0579, electronic ISSN 1536-075X) is part of The Jossey-Bass Higher and Adult Education Series and is published quarterly by Wiley Subscription Services, Inc., A Wiley Company, at Jossey-Bass, One Montgomery Street, Suite 1200, San Francisco, California 94104-4594 (publication number USPS 098-830). POSTMASTER: Send address changes to New Directions for Institutional Research, Jossey-Bass, One Montgomery Street, Suite 1200, San Francisco, California 94104-4594.

INDIVIDUAL SUBSCRIPTION RATE (in USD): $89 per year US/Can/Mex, $113 rest of world; institutional subscription rate: $341 US, $381 Can/Mex, $415 rest of world. Single copy rate: $29. Electronic only–all regions: $89 individual, $341 institutional; Print & Electronic–US: $98 individual, $410 institutional; Print & Electronic–Canada/Mexico: $98 individual, $450 institutional; Print & Electronic–Rest of World: $122 individual, $484 institutional.

EDITORIAL CORRESPONDENCE should be sent to John F. Ryan at jfryan@uvm.edu.

New Directions for Institutional Research is indexed in Academic Search (EBSCO), Academic Search Elite (EBSCO), Academic Search Premier (EBSCO), CIJE: Current Index to Journals in Education (ERIC), Contents Pages in Education (T&F), EBSCO Professional Development Collection (EBSCO), Educational Research Abstracts Online (T&F), ERIC Database (Education Resources Information Center), Higher Education Abstracts (Claremont Graduate University), Multicultural Education Abstracts (T&F), Sociology of Education Abstracts (T&F).

Cover design: Wiley
Cover Images: © Lava 4 images | Shutterstock

Microfilm copies of issues and chapters are available in 16mm and 35mm, as well as microfi che in 105mm, through University Microfilms, Inc., 300 North Zeeb Road, Ann Arbor, Michigan 48106-1346.

www.josseybass.com

THE ASSOCIATION FOR INSTITUTIONAL RESEARCH (AIR) is the world's largest professional association for institutional researchers. The organization provides educational resources, best practices, and professional development opportunities for more than 4,000 members. Its primary purpose is to support members in the process of collecting, analyzing, and converting data into information that supports decision making in higher education.

CONTENTS

EDITORS' NOTES

Seven years ago, *New Directions for Institutional Research* published the volume *Using Quantitative Data to Answer Critical Questions* (Stage, 2007). In that volume, a group of quantitative researchers sought to differentiate their approaches to quantitative research from more traditional positivistic and postpositivistic approaches. The term "quantitative criticalists" described researchers who used quantitative methods to represent educational processes and outcomes to reveal inequities and to identify perpetuation of systematic inequities. The term also included researchers who questioned models, measures, and political processes in order to ensure equity when describing educational experiences. These scholars resisted *traditional* quantitative research motivations that sought solely to confirm theory and explain processes. Kincheloe and McLaren's (1994) description of critical work was useful as grounding:

- Thought is mediated by socially and historically created power relations.
- Facts cannot be isolated from values.
- The relationship between concept and object is never fixed and is often socially mediated.
- Language is central to the formation of subjectivity.
- Certain groups in society hold privilege over others that is maintained if subordinates accept their status as natural.
- Oppression has many faces that must be examined simultaneously.
- Mainstream research practices generally reproduce class, race, and gender oppression.

In the wake of the 2007 publication, there was an increase in the explicit use of critical approaches in quantitative higher education journal articles, dissertations, and other publications, although there were also several examples of resistance to this attempt. Overall though, there was enough continued interest at conferences and through informal conversations to provide the impetus for us to revisit the topic in print. Our recent *New Directions for Institutional Research* volume (No. 158, Stage & Wells, 2014), *New Scholarship in Critical Quantitative Research—Part I: Studying Institutions and People in Context*, was the first step in that direction. That volume provided an expanded conceptualization of the tasks that critical quantitative inquiry addresses to include the need to conduct culturally relevant research by studying institutions and people in context.

This final volume continues where that one left off, examining the current state of critical quantitative inquiry and looking to its use in the future.

Specifically, this volume aims to apply the critical quantitative paradigm to new populations and new approaches, while acknowledging the challenges that accompany it. In the first two chapters, authors propose ways that critical quantitative perspectives can be useful in studying American Indian and Alaska Native students as well as college students with disabilities. These are populations that are not only underserved in college but are underrepresented in institutional and higher education research as well.

Chapters 3, 4, and 5 have authors proposing a critical quantitative paradigm alongside the use of cutting-edge methods and approaches, pointing out the power as well as the dangers of doing so. Big data, person-centered approaches (rather than variable-centered approaches), and social network analysis are all presented as methods than can be leveraged critically to improve equity and outcomes for oppressed and marginalized groups in college.

In Chapter 6, a critical quantitative project is used as an example to highlight the tensions and dangers in this type of work, cautioning and yet encouraging researchers about the approach. Especially useful in this chapter are thoughts about the ways that qualitative and quantitative researchers, each with critical aims, can work productively together.

In the final chapter, we respond to each of the subsequent chapters and look back over the two-volume series. In doing so, we see where this type of work has come in the past decade and propose where this type of research may go in the future. We ultimately challenge institutional and higher education researchers to both expand and critique this growing body of work by generating new ways of thinking about the broad array of populations participating in and served by higher education while keeping in mind the goals of revealing inequity, challenging marginalization, and helping all students to succeed.

Ryan S. Wells
Frances K. Stage
Editors

References

Kincheloe, J. L., & McLaren, P. L. (1994). Rethinking critical theory and qualitative research. In N. Denzin & Y. Lincoln (Eds.), *Handbook of qualitative research* (pp. 138–157). London, UK: Sage.

Stage, F. K. (Ed.). (2007). *New Directions for Institutional Research: No. 133. Using quantitative data to answer critical questions.* San Francisco, CA: Jossey-Bass.

Stage, F. K., & Wells, R. S. (Eds.). (2014). *New Directions for Institutional Research: No. 158. New scholarship in critical quantitative research—Part 1: Studying institutions and people in context.* San Francisco, CA: Jossey-Bass.

RYAN S. WELLS *is an associate professor of higher education in the Department of Educational Policy, Research, and Administration at the University of Massachusetts Amherst.*

FRANCES K. STAGE *is a professor of higher and postsecondary education in the Department of Administration, Leadership, and Technology at New York University.*

NEW DIRECTIONS FOR INSTITUTIONAL RESEARCH • DOI: 10.1002/ir

1

This chapter discusses issues and challenges encountered in using large-scale data sets to study educational experiences and subsequent outcomes for American Indian and Alaska Native (AI/AN) students. In this chapter, we argue that the linguistic and cultural diversity of Native peoples, coupled with the legal and political ways in which education has been used to acculturate and assimilate them, makes it imperative that a full range of social, cultural, and demographic variables be collected and that these data be analyzed, using a theory of change that emphasizes the strengths of AI/AN students and their communities rather than their perceived deficits. We envision this theory of change espousing the use of data to critically unpack and respond to the role of language and culture in shaping pathways to success in education and beyond for AI/AN students. We conclude with recommendations for constructing and analyzing large-scale data sets to better represent the diversity of cultures and experiences among AI/AN students.

Use of Large-Scale Data Sets to Study Educational Pathways of American Indian and Alaska Native Students

Susan C. Faircloth, Cynthia M. Alcantar, Frances K. Stage

Today nearly 3 million people in the United States, slightly less than 1% of the total population, identify as American Indian or Alaska Native (AI/AN) (Norris, Vines, & Hoeffel, 2012). Although often grouped together for ease of reporting and analyzing quantitative data, it is important to recognize that American Indians and Alaska Natives are in fact two distinct cultural groups, each encompassing its own unique cultures, histories, and languages (Caldwell et al., 2005). While combining American Indians and Alaska Natives provides useful data, it can also serve to mask important social and economic differences that significantly impact the overall well-being and life outcomes of individuals from these two groups.

As researchers, we are particularly interested in the ways in which data are collected and analyzed to describe and explain the educational experiences and subsequent academic outcomes for AI/AN students from

NEW DIRECTIONS FOR INSTITUTIONAL RESEARCH, no. 163 © 2015 Wiley Periodicals, Inc.
Published online in Wiley Online Library (wileyonlinelibrary.com) • DOI: 10.1002/ir.20083

prekindergarten through postgraduate work (PK–20), institutionally as well as nationally. We situate this discussion within the larger domain of the social and institutional characteristics and the aims of elementary, secondary, and postsecondary education. While some practitioners and researchers (e.g., Tinto, 1987) use models of college success that emphasize students' individual integration into college, both socially and academically, this notion has been challenged by other scholars who study the success of Native[1] students in higher education (e.g., Pavel & Inglebret, 2007; Shotton, Lowe, & Waterman, 2013; Tierney, 1992). These scholars argue that rather than expecting AI/AN students to leave their cultures behind once they have entered institutions of higher education, these institutions must provide culturally relevant experiences for these students, thereby enabling them to be both academically and culturally successful.

This potential tension between students' Indigenous cultures and the cultures of the institutions of higher education in which they are enrolled raises a number of questions regarding how institutions measure student success when implementing culturally relevant practices and pedagogies aimed at academically and socially engaging students. Other questions include: What are the common challenges to examining student success for AI/AN students? How can we examine the educational pathways of AI/ANs in order to identify their strengths and to determine areas in need of support?

In response to these and other questions, this chapter makes the case for the use of a critical quantitative approach to the use of large-scale national data sets to study the educational pathways and subsequent outcomes of AI/AN students. Research on academic success and postsecondary attainment is typically focused on either the kindergarten to grade 12 or postsecondary education system rather than connecting the PK–20 educational pathways of students. However, we recognize that education does not occur in a vacuum, and the educational conditions students encounter in elementary and secondary school serve to shape their aspirations, expectations, and eventual success along the pathway to college. In response, this chapter considers ways in which both PK–12 and postsecondary data sets together may be utilized to better understand the educational conditions and subsequent academic outcomes for Native students, as well as the challenges of using these data to study a culturally distinct, diverse, and historically marginalized student group.

We begin by reviewing the educational contexts in which AI/AN students attend school, followed by an overview of some of the PK–12 and postsecondary national data sets that include sufficient numbers of Native students, schools, and staff, primarily through the use of oversampling, to allow for quantitative analysis. We then discuss some of the limitations of these data and ways in which a critical quantitative approach may help to overcome these limitations. We conclude with recommendations for future research and implications for practice.

State of Education for American Indians and Alaska Natives

Any meaningful examination of the educational conditions and subsequent academic outcomes for American Indians and Alaska Natives requires, at minimum, a basic understanding of their sociopolitical history as it relates to education. Historically, education has been used as a means to civilize and Christianize Indigenous peoples worldwide (Deyhle & Swisher, 1997), resulting in the loss of Indigenous languages and, some would argue, cultures of many Indigenous groups, including those in the United States (Faircloth, 2009). One of the things that is unique about the education of Indigenous peoples in the United States is that many of these peoples' ancestors ceded lands to the U.S. government in exchange for the provision of health, education, and basic well-being, provisions that have, more often than not, gone lacking.

Today, the majority (approximately 93%) of AI/AN students attend public schools while the remainder attend schools operated or funded by the Bureau of Indian Education and tribes, and a smaller percentage attend private schools (DeVoe & Darling-Churchill, 2008). Regardless of where they are educated, many AI/AN students experience cultural incongruence between home and school (Chrisjohn, Towson, & Peters, 1988; Lomawaima, 1995; Powers, Potthoff, Bearinger, & Resnick, 2003; Suina, 2001), making it difficult for them to reconcile their Indigenous language and culture with the Westernized academic culture of schools. Unfortunately, many of those who do succeed in school and go on to graduate are still unable to attend college due to either a real or perceived lack of access to necessary financial aid and other resources (e.g., Tierney, Sallee, & Venegas, 2007).

The lack of financial resources is due in large part to high rates of poverty among AI/AN persons. For example, nearly one third (31%) attend high-poverty schools (Ross et al., 2012), and 40% of American Indian children live at or below the poverty level (Children's Defense Fund, 2014). Poverty is especially concentrated in homes with female heads of household, with 53% of American Indian children who reside in homes with female heads of household also living in poverty. This is an important point given the relationship between poverty and academic performance and the fact that students from lower socioeconomic statuses tend to perform more poorly in school than do their peers from higher socioeconomic statuses (e.g., Duncan, Yeung, Brooks-Gunn, & Smith, 1998; Sirin, 2005).

Although many AI/AN students do graduate from high school and go on to college, a disproportionate number do not pursue postsecondary education. Data indicate only 18% of all American Indian children have parents with a bachelor's degree or higher compared to 59% of Asians, 44% of Whites, 20% of Blacks, and 16% of Latinos (Ross et al., 2012). These findings are important given the relationship between degree attainment and the potential to earn higher wages, with those graduating from college often earning more than those who do not (Faircloth & Tippeconnic, 2010). What is equally troubling is that more than half of those AI/AN students who go to college end up not graduating (Knapp, Kelly-Reid, & Ginder, 2012). This raises questions about the factors that account for student retention and graduation, as well as those for student aspirations to attend college.

Data from the 2009 National Indian Education Study (Mead, Grigg, Moran, & Kuang, 2010) indicate that 57% of American Indian eighth graders who participated in this study aspired to attend college; however, the 2011 National Indian Education Study found that 63% of AI/AN eighth graders who were surveyed had not met with their high school counselor to discuss their classes or their plans following high school (National Center for Education Statistics, 2012). This suggests a disconnect between AI/AN students' aspirations and their preparation for college. This failure to seek college counseling may also help to explain Ross et al.'s (2012) finding that only 24% of American Indian males and 33% of American Indian females between the ages of 18 and 24 are enrolled in postsecondary education, at the undergraduate or graduate level. This is the lowest rate of college attendance of all racial/ethnic groups, with 43% of White males and 51% of White females, 31% of Black males and 42% of Black females, and 26% of Latino males and 35% of Latina females attending college. An analysis of Integrated Postsecondary Education Data System (IPEDS) data also showed that American Indian students earned less than 0.8% of all associate's and bachelor's degrees in the 2008–2009 academic year (Stage, Lundy-Wagner, & John, 2013). While 0.8% may not seem so different from the population percentage of 1%, it suggests a 20% lower achievement rate within the population. In other words, while AI/AN students represent 1% of the population, they earn only 0.8%, or 80% of their share, of the college degrees earned in the United States. In contrast, if Whites, who make up approximately 73% of the population, earned 0.2% less than their 73% representation, the difference would be almost meaningless.

Critical Approach to the Study of American Indian and Alaska Native Students

As mentioned earlier in this chapter, the historical, societal, and political marginalization of American Indians and Alaska Natives has rendered them, in many cases, invisible to those within the academic arena (Shotton et al., 2013). Critical quantitative approaches are needed to reverse this trend. As Stage (2007) has argued, "When models do not accurately reflect a given population's experiences, the task is to pose alternatives to those models. Rather than focus on explanation, or fairness, [the modeling] focuses on equity concerns that can often be highlighted through analysis of large data sets" (p. 9). The Tinto (1987) model is a good case in point. This model forms the basis of much current research on college student success. It was originally developed in the 1970s from studies of students enrolled in elite colleges. More recently, scholars have challenged aspects of the model and searched for culturally relevant variables for particular student groups (Brayboy, Fann, Castagno, & Solyom, 2012; Harper & Hurtado, 2007; Hurtado & Ponjuan, 2005). Unfortunately, many of these variables are absent from existing large-scale data sets used to examine the educational conditions and subsequent outcomes of students in PK–20.

Large-Scale National Education Data Sets

The federal government has developed a collection of hundreds of national data sets, 32 of which are education data sets managed by the National Center for Education Statistics (NCES). Researchers use these national data sets to make inferences about populations and institutions, and policy makers have used these results to inform policy and practice. Thus it is imperative that all racial and ethnic groups be represented within these data sets. Unfortunately, because of the small sample size of AI/AN students in these data sets, studies often (a) exclude AI/AN students, (b) group them as "Other" or as students who identify as multiracial, or (c) fail to report any outcomes for this group after analysis because low numbers resulted in nonsignificant findings and/or low effect sizes.

Equally important is the fact that in the recent past, no national-level data were required to be collected for AI/AN students. For example, prior to 2003, the annual report commissioned by the U.S. Department of Education, *The Condition of Education*, did not report on AI/AN students. In 2003, the U.S. Office of Management and Budget (OMB), which "is responsible for the standards that govern the categories used to collect and present federal data on race and ethnicity" (Kena et al., 2014, p. vi), revised its guidelines to include the reporting of at least five racial categories including AI/ANs. Unfortunately, the lack of data prior to 2003 continues to limit longitudinal analysis of the educational pathways of AI/AN students.

In spite of this failure to systematically include AI/AN students in the bulk of the large-scale education data sets, a limited number of data sets have been constructed that do include AI/AN children, youth, and adults. In the following section, we describe some of these data sets and selected analyses that have been conducted involving AI/AN specific data. The focus here is on PK–20 education for American Indians and Alaska Natives.

PK–12 National Data Sets.   Four national data sets have included sufficient numbers of AI/AN children, youth, and/or adults in PK–12 to allow for disaggregation and analysis of data. These data sets are discussed in brief next.

Early Childhood Longitudinal Study, Birth Cohort (ECLS-B). The ECLS-B contains an oversample of American Indian and Alaska Native children from 2001 to 2006 (oversampling involves creating a sample of respondents that exceeds their actual representation in the population; see

Table 1.1. Early Childhood Longitudinal Study Data Set, by Percentage Race/Ethnicity

	ECLS-B: 2001–2002	ECLS-K: 1998–1999	ECLS-K: 2010–2011
Total (N)	10,700	21,400	18,200
White	41.12%	55.08%	46.65%
American Indian/Alaska Native	**2.80%**	**0.59%**	**2.09%**
Asian	11.21%	1.33%	7.51%
Native Hawaiian/Other Pacific Islander	0.47%	0.45%*	1.23%
Black/African American	15.89%	3.66%	17.71%
Hispanic/Latino	20.56%	4.10%	21.02%
Other/More than one race	~7.94%	0.71%	3.30%

Data sources: U.S. Department of Education, National Center for Education Statistics, Early Childhood Longitudinal Study, Birth Cohort (ECLS-B; 2001–2002, original data collected for children at 9 months of age); and the Early Childhood Longitudinal Study, Kindergarten Cohort (ECLS-K; 1998–1999 & 2011).
*Only Pacific Islanders. Data obtained from personal communication with project officer, October 1, 2014

Table 1.1).[2] This study tracks children from birth through entry into school and by collecting data on individual health, development, care, and education of children from birth through kindergarten entry. Using these data, Halle et al. (2009) found differences in cognitive development, as well as health disparities, between AI/AN children and their non-Native peers, as early as 9 months of age.

Early Childhood Longitudinal Study, Kindergarten Cohort (ECLS-K). The ECLS-K tracks students from kindergarten through eighth grade, in both public and private schools.[2] The ECLS-K includes data from teachers, parents/families, and schools (Table 1.1). There are currently two iterations of this study, one begun in 1998–1999 and another begun in 2010–2011. Although AI/AN students were not oversampled in these data sets, they are included in sufficient numbers to allow for statistical analysis. For example, using data from the ECLS-K (1998–1999), Hibel, Faircloth, and Farkas (2008) found that AI/AN students' referral and placement into special education could be predicted in kindergarten, based in large part on these children's scores on standardized achievement tests in reading and math. This analysis indicated that those students who performed poorly on the selected achievement tests were more likely to receive special education services in the early grades. Also drawing on the ECLS-K (1998–1999), Marks and Coll (2007) utilized latent growth modeling to examine similarities and differences in the academic preparedness and related characteristics of kindergarten students from different racial/ethnic groups. They found that AI/AN students who came to school academically prepared did much better in school than did their peers who are less ready to learn.

National Assessment of Educational Progress (NAEP).   The NAEP is the largest nationally representative data set in the United States.[3] It includes data from assessments in math, reading, science, writing, the arts, civics, economics, geography, and U.S. history for students in grades 4, 8, and 12. In 2014, the NAEP also assessed students in technology and engineering literacy. Utilizing data from the 2007 administration of the NAEP, López, Heilig, and Schram (2013) found that culturally relevant curriculum and teaching practices had a potentially negative effect on AI/AN students' achievement on standardized measures of reading and math in grades 4 and 8. In another study, Fischer and Stoddard (2013) used NAEP data supplements to examine the academic achievement of American Indian students. They found that family and school characteristics were strongly related to differences in achievement between AI/AN students and their peers. This study also yielded a number of interesting findings related to students' identification as AI/AN and schools' identification of these students' race/ethnicity. In many cases, these two identities differed.

National Indian Education Study (NIES).   First conducted in 2005, the NIES was commissioned by the Office of Indian Education, within the U.S. Department of Education, and the NCES. This study was initially mandated by a 2004 presidential executive order, "recogniz[ing] the unique educational and culturally related academic needs of American Indian and Alaska Native students consistent with the unique political and legal relationship of the Federal Government with tribal governments" (Executive Order No. 13336, 2004, p. 25295). The NIES includes data from two surveys—the NAEP and a separate survey aimed at better understanding the extent to which schools incorporate culturally relevant teaching and learning practices. In 2011, 5,500 AI/AN students in the fourth grade and 4,100 Native students in the eighth grade completed the reading assessment, while 5,400 fourth graders and 4,200 eighth graders completed the math assessment.[4] Although data from the NIES is available as both public and restricted use data, the bulk of publications (e.g., Moran, Rampey, Dion, & Donahue, 2008; Rampey, Lutkus, Weiner, & Rahman, 2006; Stancavage et al., 2006) resulting from these data have been commissioned by NCES as reports of the initial findings of this study, utilizing descriptive statistics, and presentation of emergent themes, rather than higher-level statistical analysis.

Schools and Staffing Survey (SASS).   The SASS collects data on the characteristics of schools and staff (i.e., teachers and school leaders) in schools across the nation.[5] Unfortunately, after the 2007–2008 administration, the SASS discontinued the inclusion of schools operated or funded by the Bureau of Indian Affairs (BIA), where approximately 8% of all American Indian students attend schools. In the last year of inclusion of BIA schools (2008), SASS included data for approximately 9,800 public schools, 180 BIA schools, 9,800 public school principals, 180 BIA principals, 47,440 public school teachers, and 750 BIA teachers.[6] Although the BIA schools were

NEW DIRECTIONS FOR INSTITUTIONAL RESEARCH • DOI: 10.1002/ir

included between 1990 and 2008, with the exception of Pavel and Curtin (1997) and Pavel, Skinner, Farris, Cahalan, Tippeconnic, and Stein (1998), few researchers have used these data to examine the overall characteristics of schools serving AI/AN students.

Postsecondary Data Sets.   Table 1.2 provides percentages from data on three NCES national postsecondary data sets by race/ethnicity. We see that in the Baccalaureate and Beyond (B&B), Beginning Postsecondary Study (BPS), National Postsecondary Student Aid Study (NPSAS), and Integrated Postsecondary Education Data System (IPEDS) databases, American Indians and Alaska Natives ranged from less than 0.5% of the sample to 0.9%. These numbers are below the widely reported 1% of college students who are American Indians or Alaska Natives. These differences may seem minor, but a lower AI/AN response rate of 0.5% in the sample means that American Indians and Alaska Natives have only half the representation in the sample of their actual population proportion, which is 1%.

Beginning Postsecondary Study (BPS).   While BPS (2004:09) oversampled for AI/AN students, response rates were relatively low (see Stage, Alcantar, & Galvan, 2013).[7] Even with the oversampling of this population, missing data were problematic. For some variables, over 50% had missing responses. Missing data in such a small sample size force the researcher to

Table 1.2. NCES National Postsecondary Data Sets, by Percentage Race/Ethnicity

	B&B: 2008–2012	BPS: 2009	NPSAS: 2012 Undergraduates	NPSAS: 2012 Graduate	NSOPF: 2004 Faculty
Total (N)	17,110	18,640	110,790	17,330	34,330
White	72.95%	61.54%	57.88%	63.59%	82.50%
American Indian/ Alaska Native	**0.42%**	**0.63%**	**0.91%**	**0.43%**	**0.40%**
Asian	5.83%	4.71%	5.60%	12.88%	6.4%[**]
Native Hawaiian/Other Pacific Islander	0.38%	0.37%	0.51%	0.55%	N/A[***]
Black/African American	8.56%	13.79%	16.09%	11.78%	5.50%
Hispanic/Latino	9.19%	14.90%	16.03%	8.72%	3.10%
Other	0.20%	1.31%	N/A[*]	N/A[*]	N/A[*]
More than one race	2.47%	2.75%	2.98%	2.04%	2.10%

Data sources: U.S. Department of Education, National Center for Education Statistics, 2012 Baccalaureate and Beyond Longitudinal Study (B&B:12); U.S. Department of Education, National Center for Education Statistics, 2009 Beginning Postsecondary Students Longitudinal Study (BPS:09); U.S. Department of Education, National Center for Education Statistics, 2004 National Study of Postsecondary Faculty (NSOPF: 04); U.S. Department of Education, National Center for Education Statistics, 2011–12 National Postsecondary Student Aid Study (NPSAS:12).
[*]"Other" not available.
[**]Asian category in NSOPF includes Pacific Islander.
[***]Native Hawaiian/Pacific Islander category included in Asian category.

identify proxy variables and hope for less missing data or use mean imputation or other techniques to save as many cases as possible for analysis. Researchers attempting to uncover unique factors related to AI/AN students' access to and success in college found their efforts stymied (Stage, Alcantar, & Galvan, 2013). While data were collected from 448 AI/AN respondents for the Beginning Postsecondary Study data set (2.4% of the total sample), several hundred had missing data on many of the individual student response measures.

National Postsecondary Student Aid Study (NPSAS).   NPSAS is a national longitudinal study that collects data about the ways in which students and families finance their postsecondary education.[8] The national sample includes funded and nonfunded students from various types of institutions (private, public, two- and four-year, undergraduate, and graduate levels). NPSAS also served as the base-year data collections for the BPS and B&B at different years. The data come from students and from administrative data. NPSAS has been collecting data since the 1990s. NPSAS has a larger overall sample size than other NCES data sets and a larger AI/AN undergraduate student sample (0.91%; see Table 1.2). A report on the national education trends of AI/AN students developed by NCES demonstrated that in the 2003–2004 school year, 82% of AI/AN full-time undergraduate students received financial aid (DeVoe & Darling-Churchill, 2008).

Integrated Postsecondary Education Data System (IPEDS).   IPEDS is an annual survey that includes all institutions that participate in the federal student financial aid programs.[9] Institutions must report on enrollment; program completion; graduation rates; faculty and staff; finances; several student and institutional indicators, such as enrollment and graduation rates; and finances and institutional prices (U.S. Department of Education, 2010). Although this data set is designed to represent the majority of colleges and universities across the United States, there are still issues with it. One issue is that difficulties exist in obtaining accurate data for small populations—thus, it is important to examine changes in numbers over time as well as the percentage of change. A second issue associated with IPEDS is that some institutions fail to report data, necessitating the imputation of data for these institutions. Finally, a remaining issue concerns the use of self-reported racial/ethnic data—often misreported for several reasons that are discussed later.

Examples of Critical Approaches Using Large Data Sets

Although these national data sets have sometimes proven problematic, researchers have examined underrepresented populations using these data sets with a critical quantitative approach. Often these national data are used to inform data derived from state- and institution-level surveys and other means of data collection. It is imperative we learn from these studies in order to inform the development, data collection, and analysis of research on AI/AN students.

Oseguera and Hwang (2014) used the Educational Longitudinal Study 2002–2006 to study college access for low-income students using a critical quantitative approach. They chose a theory that reflected experiences of low-income populations as well as particular variables that were relevant to low-income students' college experiences. Because the sample size was already low, they used multiple techniques to impute values (Oseguera & Hwang, 2014). By using more complex imputation techniques, they were able to reduce loss of cases through missing data.

Stage, Alcantar, and Galvan (2013) used the BPS (2004:09) to study AI/AN student success in college, defined by months enrolled, degree expectations, and persistence or degree attainment. Using a critical approach, they included measures of high school academics; characteristics of college including distance from home and percentage minority enrollment; remedial course taking in college; and participation in college activities, academic support groups, and college study groups. Variables such as high school academic course taking, college distance from home, personal goals such as becoming a community leader, and engagement on campus—meeting or talking with faculty and advisors, club participation, community service, and study groups—all influenced outcomes positively. Additionally, given the relatively low graduation rate for AI/AN students, the additional measures to model persistence, total months attended, and highest degree expected proved useful.

Finally, in Chapter 2, Vaccaro, Kimball, Wells, and Ostiguy make suggestions about interpretation of data with large data sets and small sample sizes. Their study of students with disabilities shared similar challenges as research with AI/AN students. Within the population of students with disabilities are many differences based on type of disability. One suggestion was to conduct multiple operationalizations to test for robust findings across multiple analyses. Several significant results for a particular variable might suggest greater validity. Additionally, the authors suggested that researchers discuss important findings, whether significant or not. For example, a variable with a large effect size but no significant influence on the outcome may still be an important variable whose effect size should be further explored and discussed.[10]

Beyond the Data.   As previously discussed, researchers have cited a number of problems associated with studies of American Indians and Alaska Natives relevant to the use of large-scale data sets (Kena et al., 2014; Ross et al., 2012). These problems include: (1) issues related to self-identification of race and ethnicity, (2) issues of tribal identity, (3) difficulty gaining access and entrée into AI/AN communities for research purposes, (4) the need for the development and use of culturally appropriate strategies for increasing AI/AN representation in large-scale data sets, and (5) a limited pool from which to draw AI/AN samples of sufficient size for large-scale data sets. These issues are discussed in brief next.

1. Who is American Indian or Alaska Native? Who gets to decide? What does it mean to be classified as American Indian? A number of issues impact whether a population identified as American Indian, Alaska Native, or Native American is included in nationally collected data sets. For example, Demmert, Grissmer, and Towner (2006) assert that when the term "Native American" is used, we often have no way of knowing whether this term is used accurately, as some individuals identify as Native American based on the fact that they were born or reside in the United States. Although individuals have the right to self-identify as any racial or ethnic group they choose, it is important to acknowledge that for Native Americans, the question of identity and tribal membership is one that is culturally and politically complex, as it is rooted in principles of tribal self-determination and local tribal control (e.g., National Congress of American Indians, n.d.). While tribes have the right to determine who their tribal members are, most national surveys allow respondents to self-report to which racial/ethnic group they belong, thereby opening the door for those who are not tribally recognized to identify as American Indian. According to the Bureau of Labor Statistics, "Research on the collection of race/ethnicity data suggests that the categorization of American Indian and Alaska Native is the least stable self-identification" (Kena et al., 2014, p. viii). In other words, individuals may self-identify in these categories inconsistently. Kena et al. (2014) also point out that the way in which questions of identity are posed can also impact the way in which individuals respond, particularly if these individuals consider themselves to be of more than one racial or ethnic group. This fact must be considered when analyzing the results of surveys and other types of data where race/ethnicity is based on self-reporting.

2. The question of identity is critical in that analysis of data from large-scale data sets lends itself to clustering respondents in such a way that the heterogeneous nature of groups, such as American Indians and Alaska Natives, may be overlooked or overshadowed (Lavelle, Larsen, & Gundersen, 2009). The question of identity is important given that there are more than 600 different state and federally recognized tribes, each with its own culture and many with their own language—as more than 200 different Native languages are still spoken today. Within each of these tribes are unique cultural and linguistic traditions, practices, and characteristics that are not easy to tease out or to explain without interacting and talking with members of these groups. By combining tribal groups into one larger catchall category, we "can sometimes mask significant differences between

subgroups" (Ross et al., 2012, p. 1). In effect, we may be masking the variables that have the greatest effect or impact on student outcomes.

3. Gaining access and entrée into AI/AN communities for the purposes of research is difficult. According to Lavelle et al. (2009), issues of "mobility, geographic dispersion, and higher proportion of non-telephone households" (p. 386) make it difficult to access many Native peoples. These issues of physical access are also complicated by larger issues of social isolation and distrust of outsiders.

4. There is an ongoing need for the development and use of culturally appropriate strategies for increasing AI/AN representation in large-scale data sets. According to Lavelle et al. (2009), there are a number of ways in which to improve AI/AN participation in large-scale studies. These include:

   a. The establishment of agreements between tribes and tribal organizations and the agency or organization conducting the research, explaining what information will be collected, how it will be used, and the ways confidential information will be protected;

   b. Formal documentation from the tribe/tribal organization supporting the study;

   c. Training in cultural awareness for those administering surveys or other means of data collection; and

   d. Involving community/tribal members in the collection of data.

   Such strategies lend themselves to creating an atmosphere in which Native students feel welcome.

5. Small sample size and the limited pool from which to draw AI/AN samples are often problematic for the development and analysis of large-scale data sets. Small sample size impacts the reliability of the data and limits the ability of researchers to analyze data in ways that are meaningful for Native students (Ross et al., 2012). Small sample sizes also result in high standard errors, thus impacting findings of statistical significance. According to Kena et al. (2014), "survey data for American Indians/Alaska Natives often have somewhat higher standard errors than data for other racial/ethnic groups. Due to large standard errors, differences that seem substantial are often not statistically significant and, therefore, not cited in the text" (p. vii). As a result, asterisks or dotted lines are often placed beside the category of American Indian/Alaska Native to indicate inability to report due to small sample sizes. The practical implications of these symbols are aptly described in the book *Beyond the Asterisk: Understanding Native Students in Higher Education* (Shotton et al., 2013). In that book, the authors call for increased data collection and analysis specific to American Indians in higher education. In addition to the recommendations by Shotton et al. (2013), Lavelle et al. (2009) recommend the use of oversampling and increasing the overall sample size, strategies that may prove cost prohibitive for some researchers.

While the research issues just described were illustrated primarily by difficulties with large national data sets, similar issues can be found in state and single institutional-level data sets. According to Demmert et al. (2006), "research on Native American achievement has mainly been small scale, non-experimental, non-longitudinal and methodologically problematic" (p. 6). Most existing studies include sample sizes smaller than 500 and focus on individual tribes or subgroups, thus limiting the ability to make between group comparisons. While small quantitative and qualitative studies have provided useful information, more large-scale work needs to be done. These and other issues suggest that caution is warranted for institutional researchers and other scholars seeking to conduct quantitative studies of AI/AN students.

Implications for Research, Policy, and Practice

It is important that institutional researchers and scholars develop an increasing awareness of these issues and address them in research design and data collection. While many examples cited above referred to national data sets, these issues remain for any quantitative analysis of data focusing on students generally by racial and ethnic subgroups, including national, state, college system, and single institution. Issues regarding sample size for institutions or state systems can be minimized by oversampling for relatively small campus populations in order to draw meaningful analyses and conclusions. For example, rather than taking a 10% sample of the entire student body, perhaps a 20% or even greater sample should be taken for smaller populations such as AI/AN students. This issue of sample size, coupled with the need to ensure the sample is representative of the population studied, is critically important. According to Demmert et al. (2006), small sample sizes "limit the types and complexity of analysis possible in trying to understand Native American achievement" (p. 5).

Challenges researchers face in conducting studies of American Indians and Alaska Natives ultimately have broad consequences for national, state, and institutional policies and practices (Lavelle et al., 2009). Analyzing data from a critical perspective offers a way to make both scholarly and practical sense of the often confounding nature of research, particularly research seeking to draw on large numbers of American Indian students. As this chapter documents, numerous dangers exist in simply mining large-scale data sets without awareness of limitations and appropriate cautions.

The concerns just listed can be remedied by developing policies and practices to ameliorate the use of culturally misaligned data. If, as researchers, we impose our own thoughts and beliefs onto the data without giving careful consideration to alternative perspectives and approaches, a cultural mismatch will result between what we purport to measure and what is actually measured in multiple ways. This issue can be minimized by (1) ensuring that constructs being assessed are culturally relevant (see

NEW DIRECTIONS FOR INSTITUTIONAL RESEARCH • DOI: 10.1002/ir

Castagno & Brayboy, 2008); (2) ensuring that researchers use valid measures and critically examine response rates, ranges, and averages to ensure accurate representation in reporting; (3) acknowledging the limitations of existing data; and (4) committing fiscal and human resources to increase the overall quality and quantity of AI/AN-specific data.

Recommendations for Future Research

As discussed earlier, there is a paucity of published quantitative research that focuses on AI/AN students. Additionally, undersampling of such students, given small population numbers, promises to slow progress. As a result, a number of important educational, social, and cultural questions remain unanswered. The focus of this chapter is on the need to engage in a more critical analysis of national, state, and institutional data.

As López et al. (2013) point out, the collection of information regarding American Indian students' cultural experiences within school is important; however, studies must also assess the extent to which students, parents, teachers, and school leaders perceive education to be academically and intellectually rigorous, the extent to which students are expected to excel academically, and the quality of education students receive. This process of assessment includes measuring the extent to which students see the importance of their Native culture(s) as well as the ways in which teachers are taught to engage in culturally relevant teaching and learning practices during their teacher preparation programs. López et al. (2013) argue:

> Without these considerations, researchers who use [studies such as] the NIES to examine how culture is related to achievement may assert that the practice is associated with lower achievement, and make policy recommendations to limit AIAN [American Indian/Alaska Native] culture—returning education for AIAN students to the 1950s policies that diminished the AIAN-focused curriculum (Tippeconnic & Swisher, 1992) or even used to justify retrogressive standards policies in US history and other subjects that neglect the history of AIAN students. (p. 534)

Finally, it is important to acknowledge that the complexity of the AI/AN population may not be fully understood by utilizing existing quantitative data without supplementing these data with qualitative data in the form of individual and group interviews, observations, and other forms of in-depth data collection and analysis. According to Hines (1993), the use of mixed methods may help to improve the overall quality of research with culturally diverse groups, such as American Indians and Alaska Natives. The use of data collection techniques that allow researchers to probe more deeply and to provide a more nuanced understanding of the educational experiences and subsequent outcomes of AI/AN students is an important point given the fact that the educational experiences and subsequent outcomes for AI/AN peoples have been shaped by more than 500 years of cultural, political, and legal subjugation, played out in part by educational systems that have attempted to save the individual by killing the Indian (e.g., Adams, 1995). For many individuals and communities, this attempt to acculturate and assimilate has resulted in historic traumas that portray education as a means of oppression rather than the great equalizer it is often heralded to be (e.g., Grande, 2004).

Critical quantitative measures, coupled with qualitative data, have the potential to assist educators and other education researchers in understanding issues such as these three: (1) the role language and culture play in shaping AI/AN students' precollege educational experiences and subsequent academic and life outcomes; (2) the disconnect between early aspirations to attend college and historically low rates of college entry, persistence, and completion; and (3) the meaning of academic success for American Indian students, their homes, schools, and communities (i.e., what does it mean to be successful to Native peoples? How does this relate to the practice of schooling at the PK–20 level?).

Need for a New Critical Theory of Change

Critical quantitative approaches to researching the educational conditions and subsequent academic outcomes of American Indian and Alaska Natives are required if we are to fully understand the educational conditions and subsequent academic outcomes of Native students. As we work to develop these approaches, we must reflect on the work of Native scholars, such as Tuck (2009), who caution against the use of what she describes as "damage-centered research" (p. 409)—research that focuses solely on what is wrong with Native peoples rather than on their strengths as well as their needs. This shift requires researchers, particularly those who engage in education research using large-scale databases, to adopt a new theory of change, one that we characterize as utilizing data to critically unpack and respond to the role of language and culture in shaping pathways to success in education and beyond. As Tuck (2009) so aptly argues, this process involves moving away from theories of change that focus on what is wrong, missing, or absent among Native students, their schools, and communities—in other words, deficit frameworks—and instead moving toward research that seeks to identify what is right with these students, their schools and communities, and what can be done to improve the culture, climate, and conditions of academic institutions in order to better enable these students to flourish both academically and culturally. Doing this requires asking hard questions about "who participates in the research, who poses the questions, how data are gathered, and who conducts the analysis" (Tuck, 2009, p. 423). All are questions that can and should be addressed through a critical quantitative approach.

Conclusion

This chapter discusses issues and challenges encountered in analyzing data, both large-scale data and smaller, institutional-level data, to study the educational experiences and outcomes for AI/AN students. Lessons from analysis of national data sets are extended to inform institutional researchers and other scholars who aim to study issues related to the educational experiences and subsequent outcomes of American Indian college students, as well as other issues at the institutional, state, and national levels. These lessons are also applicable to student affairs practitioners who are interested in improving college access and educational attainment among AI/AN students. Issues discussed include the dangers of using ill-suited or irrelevant models that do not fully capture or take into consideration the full linguistic and cultural diversity of AI/AN students, the lack of salient measures, and small sample sizes. The authors conclude with recommendations for constructing and analyzing large-scale data sets to better represent the diversity of cultures and experiences found among AI/AN students.

Notes

1. The term "Native American" is often used interchangeably with the term "American Indian/Alaska Native."
2. For additional information, see http://nces.ed.gov/ecls/index.asp
3. For additional information, see http://nces.ed.gov/nationsreportcard/about/
4. For additional information regarding the sample composition of the NIES, see http://nces.ed.gov/nationsreportcard/nies/faq.aspx#participated
5. For additional information regarding the SASS, see http://nces.ed.gov/surveys/sass/
6. Data obtained from http://nces.ed.gov/surveys/sass/methods0708.asp and http://nces.ed.gov/pubs2009/2009324/
7. For additional information regarding the BPS, see http://nces.ed.gov/surveys/bps/
8. For additional information regarding the NPSAS, see http://nces.ed.gov/surveys/npsas/
9. For additional information on IPEDS, see http://nces.ed.gov/ipeds/datacenter/
10. Measures and results should be examined whether significant or nonsignificant. Research on testing and assessments have pointed out the importance of examining the consequential validity of measures and results (Messick, 1979). Consequential validity is the social consequences of using certain measures and results. One area to be particularly cautious with is the relationships among sample size, significance level, and effect size. Large sample sizes can produce statistically significant results with low and meaningless or irrelevant effect sizes. Conversely, very small samples can produce large effect sizes but statistically nonsignificant. The potential impact of small sample size is particularly important for studies on the educational outcomes of AI/AN students. Often these studies have small sample sizes and render nonsignificant results, yet the results are useful for policy and practice. Large effect sizes should be discussed as possible factors to be explored in future research.

NEW DIRECTIONS FOR INSTITUTIONAL RESEARCH • DOI: 10.1002/ir

References

Adams, D. W. (1995). *Education for extinction: American Indians and the boarding school experience, 1875–1928.* Lawrence, KS: University Press of Kansas.

Brayboy, B. M. J., Fann, A. J., Castagno, A. E., & Solyom, J. A. (2012). *Postsecondary education for American Indian and Alaska Natives: Higher education for nation building and self-determination* [ASHE Higher Education Report, 37(5)]. San Francisco, CA: Jossey-Bass.

Caldwell, J. Y., Davis, J. D., Du Bois, B., Echo-Hawk, H., Erickson, J. S., Goins, R. T., . . . Stone, J. B. (2005). Culturally competent research with American Indians and Alaska Natives: Findings and recommendations of the first symposium of the work group on American Indian Research and Program Evaluation Methodology. American Indian and Alaska Native Mental Health Research. *Journal of the National Center, 12*(1), 1–21. Retrieved from http://files.eric.ed.gov/fulltext/EJ742928.pdf

Castagno, A. E., & Brayboy, B. M. J. (2008). Culturally responsive schooling for Indigenous youth: A review of the literature. *Review of Educational Research, 78*(4), 941–993.

Children's Defense Fund. (2014). *The state of America's children.* 2014. Retrieved from http://www.childrensdefense.org/zzz-child-research-data-publications/data/2014-soac .pdf

Chrisjohn, R., Towson, S., & Peters, M. (1988). Indian achievement in school: Adaptation to hostile environments. In J. W. Berry, S. H. Irvine, & E. B. Hunt (Eds.), *Indigenous cognition: Functioning in cultural context* (pp. 257–283). Dordrecht, the Netherlands: Marinus Nijhoff.

Demmert, W. G., Grissmer, D., & Towner, J. (2006). A review and analysis of the research on Native American students. *Journal of American Indian Education, 45*(3), 5–23.

DeVoe, J. F., & Darling-Churchill, K. E. (2008). *Status and trends in the education of American Indians and Alaska Natives: 2008* (NCES 2008-084). Washington, DC: National Center for Education Statistics, Institute of Education Sciences, U.S. Department of Education.

Deyhle, D., & Swisher, K. (1997). Research in American Indian and Alaska Native education: From assimilation to self-determination. *Review of Research in Education, 22*, 113–194.

Duncan, G. J., Yeung, W. J., Brooks-Gunn, J., & Smith, J. R. (1998). How much does childhood poverty affect the life chances of children? *American Sociological Review, 63*(3), 406–423.

Executive Order No. 13336 of April 30, 2004, American Indian and Alaska Native Education. *Federal Register, 69*(87). Retrieved from http://www.ed.gov/edblogs/whiaiane /files/2012/04/Executive-Order-133361.pdf

Faircloth, S. C. (2009). Re-visioning the future of education for Native youth in rural schools and communities. *Journal of Research in Rural Education, 24*(9), 1–4. Retrieved from http://jrre.vmhost.psu.edu/wp-content/uploads/2014/02/24-9.pdf

Faircloth, S. C., & Tippeconnic, J. W., III. (2010). The dropout/graduation crisis among American Indian and Alaska Native students: Failure to respond places the future of Native peoples at risk. *Civil Rights Project/Proyecto Derechos Civiles.* Retrieved from http://civilrightsproject.ucla.edu/research/k-12-education/school-dropouts/the-dropo ut-graduation-crisis-among-american-indian-and-alaska-native-students-failure-to-r espond-places-the-future-of-native-peoples-at-risk/faircloth-tippeconnic-native-amer ican-dropouts.pdf

Fischer, S., & Stoddard, C. (2013). The academic achievement of American Indians. *Economics of Education Review, 36*, 135–152. doi:10.1016/j.econedurev.2013.05.005

Grande, S. (2004). *Red pedagogy: Native American social and political thought.* Lanham, MD: Rowman and Littlefield.

Halle, T., Forry, N., Hair, E., Perper, K., Wandner, L., Wessel, J., & Vick, J. (2009). *Disparities in early learning and development: Lessons from the early childhood longitudinal study—birth cohort (ECLS-B)*. Washington, DC: Child Trends.

Harper, S. R., & Hurtado, S. (2007). Nine themes in campus racial climates and implications for institutional transformation. In S. R. Harper & L. D. Patton (Eds.), *New Directions for Student Services: No. 120. Responding to the realities of race on campus* (pp. 7–24). San Francisco, CA: Jossey-Bass.

Hibel, J., Faircloth, S. C., & Farkas, G. (2008). Unpacking the placement of American Indian and Alaska Native students in special education programs and services in the early grades: School readiness as a predictive variable. *Harvard Educational Review, 78*(3), 498–528.

Hines, A. M. (1993). Linking qualitative and quantitative methods in cross-cultural survey research: Techniques from cognitive science. *American Journal of Community Psychology, 21*(6), 729–746.

Hurtado, S., & Ponjuan, L. (2005). Latino educational outcomes and the campus climate. *Journal of Hispanic Higher Education, 4*(3), 235–251.

Kena, G., Aud, S., Johnson, F., Wang, X., Zhang, J., Rathbun, A., . . . Kristapovich, P. (2014). *The condition of education 2014* (NCES 2014-083). Washington, DC: U.S. Department of Education, National Center for Education Statistics. Retrieved from http://nces.ed.gov/pubs2014/2014083.pdf

Knapp, L. G., Kelly-Reid, J. E., & Ginder, S. A. (2012). *Enrollment in postsecondary institutions, Fall 2011; Financial statistics, fiscal year 2011; and graduation rates, selected cohorts, 2003–2008: First look (Provisional Data)* (NCES 2012-174 rev). Washington, DC: U.S. Department of Education, National Center for Education Statistics. Retrieved from http://www.cop.wsu.edu/docs/r_d_docs/enrollment_postsecondary_fall11.pdf

Lavelle, B., Larsen, M. D., & Gundersen, C. (2009). Research synthesis: Strategies for surveys of American Indians. *Public Opinion Quarterly, 73*(2), 385–403.

Lomawaima, K. T. (1995). Educating Native Americans. In J. A. Banks & C. A. McGee Banks (Eds.), *The handbook of research on multicultural education* (pp. 331–345). New York, NY: Macmillan.

López, F. A., Heilig, J. V., & Schram, J. (2013). A story within a story: Culturally responsive schooling and American Indian and Alaska Native achievement in the national Indian education study. *American Journal of Education, 119*(4), 513–538.

Marks, A. K., & Coll, C. G. (2007). Psychological and demographic correlates of early academic skill development among American Indian and Alaska Native youth: A growth modeling study. *Developmental Psychology, 43*(3), 663–674. doi:10.1037/0012-1649.43.3.663

Mead, N., Grigg, W., Moran, R., & Kuang, M. (2010). *National Indian education study 2009—Part II: The educational experiences of American Indian and Alaska Native students in grades 4 and 8* (NCES 2010-463). Washington, DC: National Center for Education Statistics, Institute of Education Sciences, U.S. Department of Education.

Messick, S. (1979). *Test validity and the ethics of assessment*. Princeton, NJ: Educational Testing Services.

Moran, R., Rampey, B. D., Dion, G., & Donahue, P. (2008). *National Indian education study, 2007. Part I: Performance of American Indian and Alaska Native students at grades 4 and 8 on NAEP 2007 reading and mathematics Assessments* (NCES 2008-457). Washington, DC: National Center for Education Statistics.

National Center for Education Statistics. (2012). *National Indian Education Study 2011* (NCES 2012-466). Washington, DC: Institute of Education Sciences, U.S. Department of Education.

National Congress of American Indians. (n.d.). *An introduction to Indian nations in the United States*. Retrieved from http://www.ncai.org/about-tribes/Indians_101.pdf

Norris, T., Vines, P. L., & Hoeffel, E. M. (2012, January). *The American Indian and Alaska Native population: 2010*. 2010 Census Briefs (C2010BR-10). Retrieved from http://www.census.gov/prod/cen2010/briefs/c2010br-10.pdf

Oseguera, L., & Hwang, J. (2014). Using large data sets to study college education trajectories. In F. K. Stage & R. S. Wells (Eds.), *New Directions for Institutional Research: No. 158. New scholarship in critical quantitative research—Part 1: Studying institutions and people in context* (pp. 37–50). San Francisco, CA: Jossey-Bass.

Pavel, D. M., & Curtin, T. R. (1997). *Characteristics of American Indian and Alaska Native education: Results from the 1990–91 and 1993–94 schools and staffing surveys*. Washington, DC: U.S. Government Printing Office, Superintendent of Documents, Mail Stop: SSOP, 20402-9328.

Pavel, D. M., & Inglebret, E. (2007). *The American Indian and Alaska Native student's guide to college success*. Westport, CT: Greenwood Press.

Pavel, D. M., Skinner, R., Farris, E., Cahalan, M., Tippeconnic, J., & Stein, W. (1998). *American Indians and Alaska Natives in postsecondary education* (NCES 98-291). Washington, DC: U.S. Department of Education, National Center for Education Statistics.

Powers, K., Potthoff, S., Bearinger, L. H., & Resnick, M. D. (2003). Does cultural programming improve educational outcomes for American Indian youth? *Journal of American Indian Education, 42*(2), 17–49.

Rampey, B. D., Lutkus, A. D., Weiner, A. W., & Rahman, T. (2006). *National Indian education study. Part I: The performance of American Indian and Alaska Native fourth- and eighth-grade students on NAEP 2005 reading and mathematics assessments statistical analysis report* (NCES 2006-463). Washington, DC: National Center for Education Statistics.

Ross, T., Kena, G., Rathbun, A., KewalRamani, A., Zhang, J., Kristapovich, P., & Manning, E. (2012). *Higher education: Gaps in access and persistence study* (NCES 2012-046). Washington, DC: U.S. Department of Education, National Center for Education Statistics, Government Printing Office.

Shotton, H. J., Lowe, S. C., & Waterman, S. J. (2013). *Beyond the asterisk: Understanding Native students in higher education*. Sterling, VA: Stylus Publishing.

Sirin, S. R. (2005). Socioeconmic status and academic achievement: A meta-analytic review of research. *Review of Educational Research, 75*(3), 417–453.

Stage, F. K. (2007). Asking critical questions using quantitative data. In F. K. Stage (Ed.), *New Directions for Institutional Research: No. 133. Using quantitative data to answer critical questions* (pp. 5–16). San Francisco, CA: Jossey-Bass.

Stage, F., Alcantar, C. M., & Galvan, D. (2013). *Pathways to college for American Indians: Factors related to access and achievement*. Paper presented at the Association for the Study of Higher Education, St. Louis, MO.

Stage, F. K., Lundy-Wagner, V. C., & John, G. (2013). Minority serving institutions and STEM: Charting the landscape. In R. Palmer, D. Maramba, & M. Gasman (Eds.), *Fostering success of ethnic and racial minorities in STEM: The role of minority serving institutions* (pp. 16–32). New York, NY: Routledge.

Stancavage, F. B., Mitchell, J. H., de Mello, V. B., Gaertner, F. E., Spain, A. K., & Rahal, M. L. (2006). *National Indian education study. Part II: The educational experiences of fourth-and eighth-grade American Indian and Alaska Native students. Statistical analysis report* (NCES 2007-454). Washington, DC: U.S. Department of Education, Institute of Education Sciences, National Center for Education Statistics. Retrieved from http://nces.ed.gov/nationsreportcard/pdf/studies/2007454.pdf

Suina, J. (2001). And then I went to school. In A. G. Melendez, M. J. Young, P. Moore, & P. Pynes (Eds.), *The multicultural Southwest: A reader* (1st ed.; pp. 91–96). Tucson: University of Arizona Press.

Tierney, W. G. (1992). *Official encouragement, institutional discouragement: Minorities in academe: The Native American experience (Interpretive perspectives on education and policy)*. Greenwich CT: Ablex Publishing.

Tierney, W. G., Sallee, M. W., & Venegas, K. M. (2007). Access and financial aid: How American Indian students pay for college. *Journal of College Admission, 197*, 14–23.

Tinto, V. (1987). *Leaving college: Rethinking the causes and cures of student attrition.* Chicago, IL: University of Chicago.

Tippeconnic, J., & Swisher, K. (1992). American Indian education. In M. C. Alkin (Ed.), *Encyclopedia of education research* (pp. 75–78). New York, NY: Macmillan Library Reference.

Tuck, E. (2009). Suspending damage: A letter to communities. *Harvard Educational Review, 79*(3), 409–427.

U.S. Department of Education. (2010). *Integrated postsecondary education data system.* Washington, DC: U.S. Department of Education. Retrieved from http://nces.ed.gov/ipeds/

SUSAN C. FAIRCLOTH is an associate professor of education in the Department of Leadership, Policy, and Adult and Higher Education at North Carolina State University.

CYNTHIA M. ALCANTAR is a research associate for the Institute for Immigration, Globalization, and Education and a doctoral student at the University of California, Los Angeles.

FRANCES K. STAGE is a professor of higher and postsecondary education in the Department of Administration, Leadership, and Technology at New York University.

NEW DIRECTIONS FOR INSTITUTIONAL RESEARCH • DOI: 10.1002/ir

In this chapter, the authors critically review the current state of quantitative research on college students with disabilities and examine the exclusion of this marginalized population from much of our research. They propose ways to conduct research that more fully accounts for this diverse and important college population. The authors argue that critical quantitative research will produce more thorough knowledge and, in turn, policies and practices that will lead to more equitable college outcomes for students with disabilities.

Researching Students with Disabilities: The Importance of Critical Perspectives

Annemarie Vaccaro, Ezekiel W. Kimball, Ryan S. Wells, Benjamin J. Ostiguy

Introduction

Since the passage of the Americans with Disabilities Act (ADA) in 1990, the number of students with disabilities entering postsecondary institutions has increased significantly (United States Government Accountability Office, 2009). Despite the fact that these students comprised roughly 11% of the postsecondary population in 2007–2008 (National Center for Education Statistics, 2012), higher education research has largely ignored students with disabilities. The small body of empirical research appears most often in specialized journals instead of the most prominent higher education publications (Peña, 2014). Critical quantitative scholars are well positioned to address the need for more research focused on this understudied population.

This chapter describes the complexity of quantitative research examining students with disabilities and outlines what higher education researchers can do to expose and address their marginalization. The structure of this chapter is inspired by Rios-Aguilar's (2014) framework for conducting critical quantitative work, which builds on Stage's (2007) conceptualization of critical quantitative research in higher education. A slightly modified version of Rios-Aguilar's list of research activities serves as headings in this

NEW DIRECTIONS FOR INSTITUTIONAL RESEARCH, no. 163 © 2015 Wiley Periodicals, Inc.
Published online in Wiley Online Library (wileyonlinelibrary.com) • DOI: 10.1002/ir.20084

chapter. In each section, we describe the challenges of doing critical quantitative research with students with disabilities and offer methodological and theoretical recommendations for navigating these hurdles. We conclude the chapter by explicating how criticalists can inform and challenge higher education policies and practices.

Employ Challenging and Enriching Theories in Multiple Disciplines

Exemplary research is thoughtfully grounded in relevant theory (Smart, 2005). This grounding includes both the conceptual framework used to structure an entire research project and more specific theories and models that shape research questions, hypotheses, instrumentation, and analyses. Well-crafted, critical quantitative research focused on students with disabilities includes a thoughtful application of critical theoretical perspectives, including critical disability theory. With roots in many critically oriented literatures (e.g., feminist, Marxist, queer, postcolonial, critical cultural studies), critical disability theory covers topics such as economic, political, physical, and social exclusion; oppressive and exclusionary language; and hegemonic ideologies that portray people with disabilities as abnormal, inferior, and unequal (Charlton, 1998, 2006; Davis, 2006; Devlin & Pothier, 2006). Critical disability studies, like other forms of critical scholarship, emphasize empowerment, agency, and social change.

In addition to utilizing appropriate conceptual frameworks, exemplary researchers also select theories and models relevant to higher education (e.g., engagement, persistence, belonging) that are best suited for the topic of study. Disability studies are multidisciplinary in nature, offering models and theories from a variety of professions and disciplines to help scholars understand complex social realities (cf. Watson, Roulstone, & Thomas, 2014). Consequently, the most illuminating models and theories for studying college students with disabilities might be found outside higher education (Kezar, 2000; Smart, 2005).

Recommendations.   Critical perspectives should shape every aspect of the research process from crafting research questions and hypotheses through analysis, interpretation, and formulation of recommendations. Exemplary researchers must understand conceptual frameworks well enough to avoid what Smart (2005) lamented as a tendency for higher education scholars to use inappropriate, incomplete, or superficial applications of theory. Moreover, scholars who study students with disabilities should make use of relevant models and theories from a variety of disciplines, including psychology, sociology, rehabilitation, biomedicine, economics, political science, and interdisciplinary fields such as disability studies, gender studies, ethnic studies, and cultural studies.

Ask Relevant Questions

As Stage (2007) noted, critical quantitative research is grounded in the questions that drive the inquiry. A research question can illuminate or further marginalize the experiences of students with disabilities. The invisibility of these students in much of the higher education literature suggests most scholars do not consider disability when they conduct studies on topics related to student success. As Davis (2006) argued, studying the experiences of nondominant populations has become commonplace (i.e., people of color, women), but people with disabilities have "been rendered more invisible than other groups" (p. xv). This is often the case in higher education when researchers compare findings by race, gender, or academic year (e.g., junior, senior), but almost never by ability. Correspondingly, we know little about this population regarding key outcomes of student success.

Even studies that focus on students with disabilities can be riddled with problems stemming from non–critically minded research questions. Critical disability scholars have argued that a hegemonic belief in the inferiority of people with disabilities plagues many North American societies (Charlton, 2006; Davis, 2006; Devlin & Pothier, 2006). It is no wonder that scholarship on students with disabilities is replete with deficit-oriented paradigms. A scan of higher education journal titles about studies including students with disabilities contain phrases such as "normal achieving," "academically struggling," "at risk," and "accommodations" (Peña, 2014). A critical analysis of these research titles might suggest that deficit paradigms prohibit us from seeing students with disabilities as fully equal.

Recommendations.   Disability is ubiquitous in higher education. Therefore, disability-informed research questions should be asked of all aspects of campus operations. We recommend institutional researchers and higher education scholars include students with disabilities in critical quantitative studies that span every functional and organizational area of higher education. These students should also be included in research about *all* important educational outcomes. Finally, we invite scholars to employ a critical disability lens as they generate research questions and hypotheses that include students with disabilities in meaningful and nondeficit ways.

Choose and/or Collect Relevant Data

When determining what data are relevant to use when studying students with disabilities, researchers should carefully consider the case as the unit from which aggregation occurs and employ methods that minimize limitations of aggregation. That is, researchers should match their data set to the question they wish to address. Much of the research about students with disabilities focuses either on very small (e.g., Dole, 2001; Stage & Milne, 1996) or very large numbers of students (e.g., Henderson, 2001;

Lombardi, Murray, & Gerdes, 2012). Small quantitative studies could be strengthened through the use of quasi-experimental or experimental designs (e.g., Lombardi, Gerdes, & Murray, 2011; Powers, Sowers, & Stevens, 1995). Research focusing on a very large number of students is capable of generating information about overall trends. However, it may yield little information about within group variation (Keller, 1998; Kezar, 2000). Studies could be strengthened by utilizing a more direct theoretical point of view (e.g., Abberley, 1987; Hutcheon & Wolbring, 2012; McClune, 2001). Both small-scale and large-scale research obscure critical aspects of the connection between disability and the postsecondary learning environment. By more carefully considering the purpose of our research and matching unit(s) of analysis to that purpose, more generalizable and actionable research about the experiences of students with disabilities can be produced.

Additional points of vulnerability to bias are found in conventional sampling and recruitment procedures that fail to account for communication and response to challenges experienced by students with disabilities (Meyers & Andresen, 2000). Critical quantitative research into the experiences of this population requires an awareness of how design choices promote or discourage participation of the target population. Poorly conceived sampling plans and modes of recruitment and administration produce biased data by systematically excluding specific subpopulations from research samples (Meyers & Andresen, 2000; Williams & Moore, 2011). For example, strict reliance on email for recruiting participants will marginalize non-English-speaking deaf students and present obstacles to those who must limit screen time due to migraine headache triggers. However, shifting to telephone recruitment is not a viable solution since that also presents obstacles to participation (Meyers & Andresen, 2000).

Once sampling concerns have been minimized, or when the researcher is selecting variables from an existing data set, there are three main sources of potential bias in the resultant data set: (1) respondents fail to answer the question the researcher intended to ask; (2) researchers fail to ask the question that they wished to have answered; and (3) researchers fail to interpret the results in a way that is contextually meaningful (Bryman, 2012). Since research about students with disabilities is particularly prone to each of these data integrity issues, we discuss each in detail.

Respondents Fail to Answer the Question the Researcher Intended to Ask. A disconnect between the question asked by the researcher and the interpretation of that question by a student taking a survey may result from the nature of disability that has physiological, psychological, and sociopolitical components. "Disability" is a contested and multifaceted term (Linton, 1998) that carries significant legal implications (Weber, 2001; West et al., 1993). Against an oppressive sociopolitical backdrop, students undergo a meaning-making process that can result in both individual and contextual identities (Dole, 2001; Jones, 1996; Troiano, 2003) that vary over time (Davis, 2006). As such, designing valid instruments may be particularly problematic since a person may have contradictory identities with regard to disability in each of these two spheres.

Research has demonstrated that college students generally have an imperfect ability to report learning and behavior (Porter, 2011, 2013). Questions about the experiences of students with disabilities are also prone to misinterpretation and error in recall. Moreover, critical disability scholars explicate the ways hegemonic messages about inferiority, deficit, and "place in society" can lead people with disabilities to internalize oppression and to adopt "false consciousness and alienation" (Charlton, 2006, p. 224). Critical scholars must be mindful about how such internalization might shape the ways students rate or rank themselves on self-reported measures.

Researchers Fail to Ask the Question That They Wished to Have Answered. Existing research hints that most faculty members have limited understanding of students with disabilities (Humphrey, Woods, & Huglin, 2011; Salzberg et al., 2002). Critical disability scholars argued that this lack of knowledge leads to a "disembodied ivory tower" (Devlin & Pothier, 2006, p. 9) where researchers without disabilities perpetuate misinformation and discrimination (Davis, 2006). In short, faculty-as-researchers may not accurately capture the experiences of this population, and the same is likely true about institutional researchers.

Furthermore, students with disabilities pose a unique challenge to construct validity. If included at all, research often utilizes disability as a singular construct, but doing so obscures significant differences *among* students with disabilities. For example, the experiences of students with learning disabilities are distinct from the experiences of students with visual impairments. Determining how to operationalize disability represents a significant professional judgment—a decision that is further complicated by disability's intersectional nature (Davis, 2006; Devlin & Pothier, 2006). Social identities such as race, class, and gender influence how students will respond to their disabilities and how society responds to them (Davis, 2006; Devlin & Pothier, 2006; Jones, 1996). Likewise, the levels and types of support available to K–12 students with disabilities are shaped by factors such as parental advocacy, school district resources, and student self-determination (Connor, 2013; Eckes & Ochoa, 2005; Murray, Lombardi, Bender, & Gerdes, 2013). The intersections of these sociopolitical, social class, and human capital resources set the stage for postsecondary experiences. As they design data collection or decide whether or not to utilize a preexisting instrument, criticalists must acknowledge disability as intersectional and situated in a sociopolitical context.

Researchers Fail to Interpret the Results in a Way That Is Contextually Meaningful. Without careful attention to the actual experiences of students with disabilities, a researcher may misinterpret students' survey responses. The use of secondary data sets exacerbates this problem. For example, the Educational Longitudinal Study (ELS) includes three distinct variables that measure whether a student has a disability: (1) one based on the student's Individualized Education Program (IEP); (2) one based on a parental response; and (3) one based on responses from mathematics and/or English teachers. The classification of a deaf student or one with autism might vary, for instance, from the IEP response to the parental response. Consequently, the results of an analysis would likely differ based on the variable employed.

For those studying the postsecondary learning environment, longitudinal data sets pose additional problems in the study of disability. A profound shift occurs during the transition to college wherein the responsibility for the identification, classification, and advocacy shifts from institutions to students (Brinckerhoff, Shaw, & McGuire, 1992). Functionally, this shift may mean data that were accurate in the K–12 context may no longer be accurate in the postsecondary learning environment.

Recommendations.   A few research strategies offer promise for assisting researchers in their quest to choose or collect relevant data. First, we believe that researchers should consider universal design principles in study design and implementation.

> Universal design means simply designing all products, buildings and exterior spaces to be usable by all people to the greatest extent possible. It is … a sensible and economical way to reconcile the artistic integrity of a design with human needs in the environment. Solutions which result in no additional cost and no noticeable change in appearance can come about from knowledge about people, simple planning and careful selection of conventional products. (Mace, Hardie, & Place, 1996, p. 2)

Although early definitions of universal design, like this one, focused heavily on architecture, space, and products, the concept has become increasingly common in education. In the educational literature, universal design typically emphasizes the creation of classroom experiences that are accessible to all (Hackman & Rauscher, 2004). We contend that universal design can also make research projects more useful, inclusive, and relevant to all.

One way to use these principles is to collect information about disability in studies that *do not* explicitly focus on disability. Such a step would produce important information about whether more commonly researched areas of higher education differ for students with disabilities. During study design, researchers should also consider the accessibility of their sampling plan, data collection method, and dissemination process. Criticalist scholars can oversample very small subpopulations likely to have unique perspectives (e.g., wheelchair users) and employ universal design principles to mitigate barriers to recruitment and response (Williams & Moore, 2011). Additionally, higher education researchers can look to other fields, such as special education, rehabilitation, and counseling, for useful approaches.

New Directions for Institutional Research • DOI: 10.1002/ir

Apply Appropriate, Rigorous, Sophisticated, and Disaggregated Analyses

After critical questions are asked and relevant data are collected, researchers must remain critical in their data analyses. In general, quantitative research with students with disabilities should be rigorous and adhere to recommended exemplary practices (Smart, 2005). One issue researchers need to consider is the consequences of aggregating students with disabilities for analyses and the implications of such decisions on critical aims of the project. Although (dis)aggregation of data for other underrepresented groups has been discussed in Chapter 1 and elsewhere (Stage, 2007), it has not been discussed meaningfully for this population. There is a need to critically examine both the impact of aggregating students with disabilities into one category (or even a few) and methods for obtaining more nuanced understandings of this heterogeneous group of students. For example, some quantitative studies simply compare students with and without disabilities, resulting in the homogenization of an extremely heterogeneous population of students.

Why is aggregation an issue at all? Quantitative researchers who conduct analyses with data containing small subsamples of students with disabilities often feel the need to aggregate or drop these subsamples, possibly leading to invisibility or misrepresentation. With small subsamples, the reliability of estimates produced in the analyses is likely to be low. Thus, researchers may not be able to make strong claims about differences between groups because the value of the estimates may be suspect. In addition, effects may be meaningful, but small samples make reaching the normative thresholds of statistical significance less likely. As such, it may be impossible to know if an effect is actually nonsignificant or if an effect cannot be detected due to a small sample. Finally, a skewed or unbalanced data set may be problematic for certain type of analyses, including classifying-oriented work like latent class analysis.

An example that highlights the complexity of aggregation comes from research currently in progress (authors Wells & Kimball) about students with disabilities in science, technology, engineering, and math (STEM) majors using the ELS. The aggregation of 2002 to 2004 ELS data from two sources (parent surveys and IEP records) yields overall and subgroup sizes that differ widely. Table 2.1 shows subsample sizes for students with and without disabilities in data collected from a parent survey, while Table 2.2 was obtained from high school IEP records. As shown, one data source shows 1,870 students with disabilities, representing 14.5% of the population, while the other reveals 1,000 students with disabilities, representing about 12% of the population.

Aggregation of data is also problematic when using either source of ELS data individually. In the rows under the raw data in both tables, we present three (problematic) ways to aggregate the data. Aggregating the data

Table 2.1. Response Options and Possible Aggregations from ELS Parental Question About Disability: "In your opinion, which of these disabilities does your tenth grader have?"

Type of Disability	Specific Learning Disabilities	Hearing Impairment	Orthopedic Impairment	Visual Impairment	Speech and Language Impairments	Mental Retardation	Emotional Disturbances	Other (e.g., Autism, Deaf-Blindness, Traumatic Brain Injury, Developmental Delay)	No Reported Disability
Subsample size	960	70	50	130	160	30	270	200	11,010
	Learning 960	Physical 240			Other 660				11,010
	Learning 960	Other (nonlearning) 910							11,010
	Learning 960	Students with disabilities 1,870							11,010

Source: Educational Longitudinal Study (ELS: 2002–04).
Notes: Values rounded to the nearest 10 in agreement with NCES restricted data license. Errors in addition are due to rounding.

Table 2.2. Categories and Possible Aggregations for ELS Variable for Disability Based on Data Taken From High School IEP Records

Type of Disability	Specific Learning Disabilities	Hearing Impairment	Orthopedic Impairment	Visual Impairment	Speech and Language Impairments	Other Health Impairment	Mental Retardation	Emotional Disturbances	Multiple Disabilities	Autism	Deaf/Blindness	Other	No reported Disability
Subsample size	690	20	<10	20	30	40	90	80	20	<10	<10	<10	7,230
	Learning 690	Physical 40		Other 270									7,230
	Learning 690	Other (nonlearning) 310											7,230
	Students with disabilities 1,000												7,230

Source: Educational Longitudinal Study (ELS: 2002–04).
Notes: Values rounded to the nearest 10 in agreement with NCES restricted data license. Errors in addition are due to rounding.

in three categories (i.e., learning, physical, other) allows for larger subpopulation sizes for analysis, and two categories (i.e., learning and nonlearning disabilities) even more so. Aggregating all students with disabilities to compare with students without disabilities gives the simplest groupings for analysis, but it is the bluntest method and loses the most information about disability type.

Although the statistical norms around and need for aggregation are understandable, there are problems with this practice in at least two ways. First, small changes in operationalization of variables (in this case aggregation of disability categories) can lead to interpretations of results that may be quite different and in danger of being overgeneralized (Wells, Lynch, & Seifert, 2011). In addition, the experiences of very small groups of students (e.g., autistic or deaf) will be hidden when they are aggregated with data from students with vastly different disabilities.

Recommendations.   Given these challenges with analyses, and particularly with (dis)aggregation, one recommendation is to collect data that oversample students with disabilities, thereby allowing robust analyses of many subgroups. If researchers are at the mercy of previously collected data, they can create groups in a manner that leads to thoughtful and nuanced understandings of students with disabilities. For example, Beginning Postsecondary Students (BPS) data have preaggregated groupings for type of disability: Mobility, Sensory, and Other. Although these classifications may be useful in some research projects, they may be inappropriate in others. Critical researchers should consider the context of their specific study before adopting any predefined groupings.

Researchers may find it useful to use a theoretical or conceptual grounding to create groups rather than using a generic default group. Based on theory or contextual understanding, researchers can make a case for why some groups of students can more appropriately be grouped together, which will, it is hoped, limit aggregation errors and invisibility of particular students with disabilities. For instance, a study that was focused on issues of disclosure, stigma, or self-concept might logically benefit from grouping students with apparent (visible) disabilities and those with nonapparent (invisible) disabilities (e.g., Olney & Brockelman, 2005).

Empirical techniques can also be used to group students in ways the data suggest are appropriate. For instance, cluster analyses can be used to create categories based on shared experiences (e.g., climate experiences) rather than grouping participants strictly by disability diagnoses (e.g., learning disability, visual impairment). Cluster analyses may also indicate that existing disability categories do not predict useful groupings based on experiences. Other types of person-centered analytic techniques will also be useful in this regard (see Chapter 4 in this volume).

In any type of grouping—empirical, theoretical, or both—the outcome being studied must be taken into consideration. For example, in some cases grouping autism with several other types of disabilities as "other disabilities" might make sense, as shown with the ELS data cited earlier (despite the problematic labeling practice of explicitly "othering" small groups of marginalized students). However, in our current study of STEM major representation, this is not the best option because past research suggests students with autism may be more likely than students without disabilities to major in STEM (Wei, Yu, Shattuck, McCracken, & Blackorby, 2013).

Another recommendation is to conduct analyses multiple ways (Wells et al., 2011). The goal with multiple operationalizations or multiple types of analyses is not to cherry-pick the versions that give the "best" results but rather to test how robust any given finding is across multiple analyses. If a finding is similar when operationalized and analyzed in different ways, it can be viewed as more valid than results produced from a single model. However, it is likely that researchers will find results from various models do not match. While such messy results may not please administrators, reviewers, or editors, presenting quantitative analyses in a way that mirrors the complexity of real life aligns with the critical aims for which we advocate.

Know How to Interpret Results

A critical interpretation of results can only occur if a study is designed to address critical questions. Beyond that, knowing how to interpret results first and foremost means knowing the methods used. For example, if one uses logistic regression, one must know how to substantively interpret logit coefficients and odds ratios.

Considerations of "significance" dominate many researchers' thinking about all quantitative methods. As such, our understandings about students with disabilities are limited to "rigorous" studies that yield statistically significant findings. Smart (2005) suggested the field of higher education has relied too much on statistical significance and not enough on substantive significance. Rios-Aguilar (2014) problematizes the notion of significance even further by using the term "educational significance" to remind researchers to consider what results "mean practically for underrepresented and marginalized groups of students' experiences and opportunities" (p. 99).

Recommendations.   We recommend that, when appropriate, quantitative criticalists push the boundaries of field and institutional norms around statistical significance when interpreting results. If the educational or substantive significance of a finding for a specific subgroup of students with disabilities is worthy of attention, the finding should be discussed regardless of whether it is statistically significant using common cut-offs such as "at the .05 level." For example, if a large difference were found in the effect of a policy on the retention of students with disabilities versus those without, but the finding was not statistically significant, it typically would be omitted from a report or paper. However, a transparent discussion about the *possible* educational or substantive significance of the finding, preferably through the lens of actual effect sizes, could still be justified from a critical perspective. There is no need to overclaim the importance of such a finding, but being silent about potential real-world significance for a marginalized group based on the rigid, often arbitrary conventions and norms of the quantitative research community (Ziliak & McCloskey, 2008) does not increase our knowledge of this important population of students. In fact, "less rigorous" yet educationally significant results may be very effective in laying the groundwork for future analyses that meet the more rigorous norms of the quantitative research community. It is precisely these small pushes by critical researchers that cumulatively may have an impact on the state of the field in researching, understanding, and supporting students with disabilities.

Inform and Challenge Existing Educational Policies and Practices

Critical scholarship is never about research for research's sake (Devlin & Pothier, 2006; Kincheloe & McLaren, 2005). Kincheloe and McLaren (2005) argue "inquiry that aspires to the name 'critical' must be connected to an attempt to confront … injustice" (p. 305). Devlin and Pothier (2006) describe the goal of critical disability theory as "a politics of transformation" (p. 12). These paradigms align nicely with Rios-Aguilar's (2014) research activities that critical quantitative scholars must engage in—informing and challenging exclusionary educational policies and practices. Yet the higher education literature contains a dearth of research about students with disabilities (Peña, 2014), making research-informed policy decisions nearly impossible. A lack of critical inquiry about students with disabilities in all realms of higher education leads practitioners to create policies and services that do not consider the needs of this growing group of students. Such exclusions have not only ethical but also potentially legal ramifications for higher education institutions.

   Recommendations.   Critical disability scholars emphasize agency and empowerment of people with disabilities (Charlton, 2006; Davis, 2006; Devlin & Pothier, 2006). Educational leaders can increase a sense of agency and empowerment in students with disabilities by encouraging the use of universal design in not only teaching, but also research. As Berger and Thanh (2004) suggest, universal design can be facilitated by cultural and organizational factors within an institution. For instance, leaders can offer special recognitions of inclusive research in university marketing materials, research award decisions, and tenure and promotion processes. Internal and external grant competitions should reward well-designed critical quantitative studies that investigate issues related to disability *and* allow people with disabilities to participate in, conduct, and benefit from research findings. Financial support for scholars using universal design could positively dispose future researchers toward utilizing these principles in their work. Further, faculty can include literature and discussions of critical quantitative methods and universal design principles in graduate research methods courses, encouraging future researchers to adopt, develop, and evaluate meaningful practices.

Emancipation is possible only when scholars recognize the privilege embedded in their roles as researchers and the potential to marginalize the perspectives and experiences of students with disabilities when using noncritical research paradigms. Higher education scholars should heed an early mantra of the disability rights movement: "Nothing about us without us" (Charlton, 1998, p. 3). The principle of beneficence suggests that study participants should benefit from their participation in the study. Students with disabilities may benefit simply from the normalization rather than stigmatization of their experience. Moreover, a critical quantitative approach that honors universal design principles will seek input and feedback from students with disabilities at all stages of research design. Students with disabilities can help researchers develop questions and validate survey instruments through focus groups, pilot studies, or cognitive interviews. Further, students with disabilities can be tapped to confirm that conclusions drawn from research are accurate and meaningful.

For decades, literature has documented that practitioners do not find the scholarly literature useful (Keller, 1985, 1998; Kezar, 2000). As such, critical researchers must strive to make study findings accessible and useful to those who create policy and work directly with students with disabilities. There is a need to close the gap between research and the practices associated with the full inclusion of this population. In this regard, offices of disability services and professional associations (e.g., the Association on Higher Education And Disability [AHEAD]) can be resources to scholars, regardless of research focus, as they begin to formulate their research questions, design their studies, and interpret data. Campus disability services professionals can also offer researchers insight into how to best capture the perspectives of diverse students via accessible research design.

If critical scholarship is intended to inspire action, then it must be accessible to practitioners who directly interact with students and to educational leaders who create policies. In her study of practitioners and research, Kezar (2000) found practitioners desired research that was timely, offered suggestions for best practices, and described solutions for daily practice dilemmas. Critical researchers should heed these suggestions when writing for both internal and external audiences. For critical scholars to inspire action, they must go beyond merely publishing in scholarly journals and presenting in scholarly conference venues (Keller, 1985). Criticalists must also speak directly to those working with students with disabilities. Key findings along with practice-based recommendations should be submitted to widely read publications (e.g., professional newsletters, magazines, and volumes such as this one). Finally, and most important, research findings should be shared with campus entities, creating a reciprocally beneficial dynamic that "help[s] to shrink the gap between equity-minded research and policy" (Stage & Wells, 2014, p. 3).

Conclusion

The application of critical quantitative practices to disability research presents a number of transformational opportunities for higher education. A persistent and important theme in the critical disability literature is that disability oppression is the result of socially imposed limitations (Shakespeare, 2006). Understood in this theoretical context, disability in higher education constitutes an important opportunity to capitalize on the strengths of critical quantitative methods by asking compelling questions and giving voice to this significant yet understudied postsecondary population.

Thoughtfully conducted, critical quantitative research about the experiences of students with disabilities can contribute to the development of institutional policies and practices that liberate rather than exclude. However, critical application of research data can occur only when critical questions are asked and data have been collected and analyzed with a design that *allows for* critical interpretation. There are a host of methodological challenges in conducting critical research with students with disabilities. While none of our recommendations offers perfect solutions to these tough methodological problems, omitting disability from higher education research or conducting noncritical inquiries with students with disabilities will only contribute to the oppression of this marginalized population. Instead, by shifting from normative methodological considerations to the transformative potential of critical quantitative work as a guiding principle, scholars can produce research that will illuminate the experiences of an underserved and underresearched population in higher education.

References

Abberley, P. (1987). The concept of oppression and the development of a social theory of disability. *Disability, Handicap & Society*, 2(1), 5–19. doi:10.1080/02674648766780021

Berger, J. B., & Thanh, D. (2004). Leading organizations for universal design. *Equity & Excellence in Education*, 37(2), 124–134. doi:10.1080/10665680490453959

Brinckerhoff, L. C., Shaw, S. F., & McGuire, J. M. (1992). Promoting access, accommodations, and independence for college students with learning disabilities. *Journal of Learning Disabilities*, 25(7), 417–429.

Bryman, A. (2012). *Social research methods* (4th ed.). New York, NY: Oxford University Press.

Charlton, J. I. (1998). *Nothing about us without us: Disability oppression and empowerment*. Berkeley, CA: University of California Press.

NEW DIRECTIONS FOR INSTITUTIONAL RESEARCH • DOI: 10.1002/ir

Charlton, J. I. (2006). The dimensions of disability oppression: An overview. In L. J. Davis (Ed.), *The disability studies reader* (2nd ed., pp. 217–227). New York, NY: Routledge.

Connor, D. J. (2013). Sink or swim: Managing the academic transition to college for students with learning disabilities. *Journal of College Student Retention: Research, Theory and Practice, 15*(2), 269–292. doi:10.2190/CS.15.2.g

Davis, L. J. (2006). Introduction. In L. J. Davis (Ed.), *The disability studies reader* (2nd ed., pp. xv–xviii). New York, NY: Routledge.

Devlin, R., & Pothier, D. (2006). Introduction: Toward a critical theory of dis-citizenship. In D. Pothier & R. Devlin (Eds.), *Critical disability theory: Essays in philosophy, politics, policy and law* (pp. 1–24). Vancouver, British Columbia: UBC Press.

Dole, S. (2001). Reconciling contradictions: Identity formation in individuals with giftedness and learning disabilities. *Journal for the Education of the Gifted, 25*(2), 103–137.

Eckes, S. E., & Ochoa, T. A. (2005). Students with disabilities: Transitioning from high school to higher education. *American Secondary Education, 33*(3), 6–20.

Hackman, H. W., & Rauscher, L. (2004). A pathway to access for all: Exploring the connections between universal instructional design and social justice education. *Equity & Excellence in Education, 37*(2), 114–123. doi:10.1080/10665680490453931

Henderson, C. (2001). *College freshmen with disabilities, 2001: A biennial statistical profile.* Washington, DC: American Council on Education.

Humphrey, M., Woods, L., & Huglin, L. (2011). Increasing faculty awareness of students with disabilities: A two-pronged approach. *Journal of Postsecondary Education and Disability, 24*(3), 255–261.

Hutcheon, E. J., & Wolbring, G. (2012). Voices of "disabled" post secondary students: Examining higher education "disability" policy using an ableism lens. *Journal of Diversity in Higher Education, 5*(1), 39–49. doi:10.1037/a0027002

Jones, S. R. (1996). Toward inclusive theory: Disability as social construction. *NASPA Journal, 33,* 347–354.

Keller, G. (1985). Trees without fruit: The problem with research about higher education. *Change, 17*(1), 7–10.

Keller, G. (1998). Does higher education research need revisions? *Review of Higher Education, 21*(3), 267–278. doi:10.1353/rhe.1998.0005

Kezar, A. J. (2000). Higher education research at the millennium: Still trees without fruit? *Review of Higher Education, 23*(4), 443–468.

Kincheloe, J. L., & McLaren, P. L. (2005). Rethinking critical theory and qualitative research. In N. K. Denzin & Y. S. Lincoln (Eds.), *The Sage Handbook of Qualitative Research* (3rd ed., pp. 303–342). Thousand Oaks, CA: Sage.

Linton, S. (1998). *Claiming disability: Knowledge and identity.* New York, NY: New York University Press.

Lombardi, A. R., Gerdes, H., & Murray, C. (2011). Validating an assessment of individual actions, postsecondary, and social supports of college students with disabilities. *Journal of Student Affairs Research and Practice, 48*(1), 104–123. doi:10.2202/1949-6605.6214

Lombardi, A. R., Murray, C., & Gerdes, H. (2012). Academic performance of first-generation college students with disabilities. *Journal of College Student Development, 53*(6), 811–826. doi:10.1353/csd.2012.0082

Mace, R. L., Hardie, G. J., & Place, J. P. (1996). *Accessible environments: Toward universal design.* Raleigh, NC: North Carolina State University, Center for Accessible Housing. Retrieved from http://www.ncsu.edu/www/ncsu/design/sod5/cud/pubs_p/docs/ACC%20Environments.pdf

McClune, B. (2001). Modular A-levels—Who are the winners and the losers? A comparison of lower-sixth and upper-sixth students' performance in linear and modular A-level physics. *Educational Research, 43*(1), 79–89. doi:10.1080/00131880010021302

Meyers, A. R., & Andresen, E. M. (2000). Enabling our instruments: Accommodation, universal design, and access to participation in research. *Archives of Physical Medicine and Rehabilitation, 81*(2) S5–S9. doi:10.1053/apmr.2000.20618

Murray, C., Lombardi, A., Bender, F., & Gerdes, H. (2013). Social support: Main and moderating effects on the relation between financial stress and adjustment among college students with disabilities. *Social Psychology of Education, 16*(2), 277–295. doi:10.1007/s11218-012-9204-4

National Center for Education Statistics. (2012). *Digest of education statistics, 2011.* U.S. Department of Education. Retrieved from nces.ed.gov/pubs2012/2012001.pdf

Olney, M. F., & Brockelman, K. F. (2005). The impact of visibility of disability and gender on the self-concept of university students with disabilities. *Journal of Postsecondary Education and Disability, 18*(1), 80–91.

Peña, E. V. (2014). Marginalization of published scholarship on students with disabilities in higher education journals. *Journal of College Student Development, 55*(1), 30–40.

Porter, S. R. (2011). Do college student surveys have any validity? *Review of Higher Education, 35*(1), 45–76. doi:10.1353/rhe.2011.0034

Porter, S. R. (2013). Self-reported learning gains: A theory and test of college student survey response. *Research in Higher Education, 54*(2), 201–226. doi:10.1007/s11162-012-9277-0

Powers, L. E., Sowers, J., & Stevens, T. (1995). An exploratory randomized study of the impact of mentoring on the self-efficacy and community-based knowledge of adolescents with severe physical challenges. *Journal of Rehabilitation, 61*(1), 33–41.

Rios-Aguilar, C. (2014). The changing context of critical quantitative inquiry. In F. K. Stage & R. S. Wells (Eds.), *New Directions for Institutional Research: No. 158. New scholarship in critical quantitative research—Part 1: Studying institutions and people in context* (pp. 95–107). San Francisco, CA: Jossey-Bass.

Salzberg, C. L., Peterson, L., Debrand, C. C., Blair, J. J., Carsey, A. C., & Johnson, A. S. (2002). Opinions of disability service directors on faculty training: The need, content, issues, formats, media, and activities. *Journal of Postsecondary Education and Disability, 15*(2), 101–114.

Shakespeare, T. (2006). The social model of disability. *The Disability Studies Reader, 2,* 197–204.

Smart, J. C. (2005). Attributes of exemplary research manuscripts employing quantitative analyses. *Research in Higher Education, 46*(4), 461–477. doi:10.1007/s11162-005-2970-5

Stage, F. K. (2007). Answering critical questions using quantitative data. In F. K. Stage (Ed.), *New Directions for Institutional Research: No. 133. Using quantitative data to answer critical questions* (pp. 5–16). San Francisco, CA: Jossey-Bass.

Stage, F. K., & Milne, N. V. (1996). Invisible scholars: Students with learning disabilities. *Journal of Higher Education, 67*(4), 426–445. doi:10.2307/2943806

Stage, F. K., & Wells, R. S. (2014). Critical quantitative inquiry in context. In F. K. Stage & R. S. Wells (Eds.), *New Directions for Institutional Research: No. 158. New scholarship in critical quantitative research—Part 1: Studying institutions and people in context* (pp. 1–7). San Francisco, CA: Jossey-Bass.

Troiano, P. F. (2003). College students and learning disability: Elements of self-style. *Journal of College Student Development, 44*(3), 404–419. doi:10.1353/csd.2003.0033

United States Government Accountability Office. (2009). *Higher education and disability: Education needs a coordinated approach to improve its assistance to schools in supporting students.* Retrieved from http://www.gao.gov/assets/300/297433.pdf

Watson, N., Roulstone, A., & Thomas, C. (Eds.). (2014). *The Routledge handbook of Disability Studies.* New York, NY: Taylor Francis.

Weber, M. C. (2001). Disability discrimination in higher education. *Journal of College and University Law, 28,* 439.

Wei, X., Yu, J., Shattuck, P., McCracken, M., & Blackorby, J. (2013). Science, technology, engineering, and mathematics (STEM) participation among college students with an autism spectrum disorder. *Journal of Autism and Developmental Disorders, 43*(7), 1539–1546. doi:10.1007/s10803-012-1700-z

Wells, R., Lynch, C., & Seifert, T. (2011). Methodological options and their implications: An example using secondary data to analyze Latino educational expectations. *Research in Higher Education, 52*(7), 693–716. doi:10.1007/s11162-011-9216-5

West, M., Kregel, J., Getzel, E. E., Zhu, M., Ipsen, S. M., & Martin, E. D. (1993). Beyond Section 504: Satisfaction and empowerment of students with disabilities in higher education. *Exceptional Children, 59*(5), 456–467.

Williams, A. S., & Moore, S. M. (2011). Universal design of research: Inclusion of persons with disabilities in mainstream biomedical studies. *Science Translational Medicine, 3*(82), 1–5.

Ziliak, S. T., & McCloskey, D. N. (2008). *The cult of statistical significance: How the standard error costs us jobs, justice, and lives.* Ann Arbor, MI: University of Michigan Press.

ANNEMARIE VACCARO *is an associate professor in the Department of Human Development and Family Studies at the University of Rhode Island.*

EZEKIEL W. KIMBALL *is an assistant professor of higher education in the Department of Educational Policy, Research, and Administration at the University of Massachusetts Amherst.*

RYAN S. WELLS *is an associate professor of higher education in the Department of Educational Policy, Research, and Administration at the University of Massachusetts Amherst.*

BENJAMIN J. OSTIGUY *is the associate director of operations for Disability Services at the University of Massachusetts Amherst.*

NEW DIRECTIONS FOR INSTITUTIONAL RESEARCH • DOI: 10.1002/ir

3

This chapter presents various definitions of big data and examines some of the assumptions regarding the value and power of big data, especially as it relates to issues of equity in community colleges. Finally, this chapter ends with a discussion of the opportunities and challenges of using big data, critically, for institutional researchers.

Using Big (and Critical) Data to Unmask Inequities in Community Colleges

Cecilia Rios-Aguilar

Business, government, scholars, and the public in general are looking at big data as the new "holy grail" to better sell products, deliver services, improve individuals' well-being, generate economic prosperity, and engage people in solving problems. Yet, while the use of big data may facilitate new approaches to tackling social problems, it also raises tough questions around complex issues such as equity, power, and exclusion. The same is true for big data and higher education institutions: What are big data? What are the value and purpose of using big data? What are the opportunities and challenges of these data for the operation of colleges and universities? What is the relationship between big data and students' outcomes?

This chapter presents and examines definitions of big data, including assumptions regarding the value and power of big data as they relate to issues of equity in community colleges. A discussion of the benefits and challenges of using big data follows, including a review of existing opportunities to design and analyze big data for college leaders and institutional researchers interested in providing college students with more opportunities to engage in college and, therefore, to succeed academically. The chapter ends with a clear message: Big data and data science alone will not solve higher education issues, and they especially will not solve them in a critical way. College leaders, scholars, and institutional researchers must consider big and critical data and how they intersect with the lives and experiences of the students they serve. That is, one of the goals of analyzing big data from a quantitative perspective should be "to conduct culturally relevant research by studying institutions and people in context" (Stage & Wells, 2014, p. 3).

NEW DIRECTIONS FOR INSTITUTIONAL RESEARCH, no. 163 © 2015 Wiley Periodicals, Inc.
Published online in Wiley Online Library (wileyonlinelibrary.com) • DOI: 10.1002/ir.20085

Big Data: Definitions and Approaches

There are many definitions of big data, which may differ depending on whether you are a business manager, a computer scientist, a financial analyst, a tech entrepreneur, or a higher education leader (Executive Office of the President, 2014). One of the most cited definitions of the term "big data" reflects the growing technological ability to capture, aggregate, and process the ever-greater *volume*, *velocity*, and *variety* of data (Ward & Barker, 2013). The National Science Foundation (NSF, 2012) has defined "big data" as "large, diverse, complex, longitudinal, and/or distributed datasets generated from instruments, sensors, Internet transactions, email, video, click streams, and/or all other digital sources available today and in the future" (p. 5). Given the importance of big data, the NSF launched a new funding program aimed at the extraction and use of knowledge from collections of large data sets in order to accelerate progress in science and engineering research. Specifically, it funds research to develop and evaluate new algorithms, statistical methods, technologies, and tools to improve data collection and management, data analytics and metrics, and e-science collaboration environments.

In the computer industry, the term has a more precise meaning. The term "big data" is applied to data sets whose size is beyond the ability of commonly used software tools to capture, manage, and process the data in a tolerable amount of time. Similarly, in business, "big data" is the term increasingly used to describe the process of applying serious computing power to extremely massive and often highly complex sets of information ("The Big Data Conundrum," 2013). But the business sector seems to be mostly concerned with the opportunities that big data provide to this particular sector. Specifically, companies (e.g., Microsoft and Intel) argue that big data offer unprecedented insight, improved decision making, and untapped resources for profit (Ward & Barker, 2013).

In the social sciences, the term "big data" is defined more comprehensively and, in some instances, more critically as a cultural, technological, and scholarly phenomenon that rests on the interplay of: (1) technology: maximizing computation power and algorithmic accuracy to gather, analyze, link, and compare large data sets, (2) analysis: drawing on large data sets to identify patterns in order to make economic, social, technical, and legal claims, and (3) mythology: the widespread belief that large data sets offer a higher form of intelligence and knowledge that can generate insights that were previously impossible, with the aura of truth, objectivity, and accuracy (Boyd & Crawford, 2012, p. 663).

It is clear that different sectors pay attention to different aspects of big data. Some put more emphasis on size, others on complexity, and others on the technologies needed to process a sizable or complex data set. While clear attention is being paid to the potential of big data, the applications of big data in higher education have, thus far, not been well documented. That is, we know very little about how big data are actually being used in post-secondary settings beyond scattered accounts of the promises of big data, and we know even less about how big data are generated. Consequently, I argue that the higher education community must adopt a definition of big data that includes technical considerations—volume, velocity, variety, and complexity—as well as nontechnical issues related to equity, power, and exclusion.

In addition to how we define big data, the higher education field must pay attention to the wide variety of potential uses and misuses of big data and of their associated predictive models, analytics, and metrics. Both raise crucial questions about the role of existing legal and ethical practices and about existing social norms and values related to the "quantification of social phenomena—the production and communication of numbers" (Espeland & Stevens, 2008, p. 401)—and, I would add, of data, models, analytics, and visuals. In other words, unprecedented computational sophistication and power certainly drive innovation and establish new regimes of measurement. Nevertheless, these capabilities and systems, most of which are not available to the majority, also alter the power dynamics among those who produce the data, those who hold the data and know how to analyze it, those who make decisions with the data, and those who are excluded from all these processes (Executive Office of the President, 2014).

In the following sections, I discuss the benefits and challenges of big data. It is important to mention that I think the higher education community should use big data and analytics and metrics that derive from them. However, I think that big data need to be designed and used in a careful and critical way. Following Stage and Wells's (2014) guidelines, the five goals of big (and critical) data in the field of higher education must be:

1. to use data to unmask inequities of various subgroups of students;
2. to question models, measures, and analytic practices;
3. to design research that is contextualized; and I would add
4. to use findings to challenge policies and practices; and
5. to provide more equitable opportunities for all students to succeed academically and in life.

Benefits of Big Data

As stated earlier, the past 10 years have yielded an explosion in the availability of data extracted from human behavior and interactions, including cell phone records with GPS tracking, search engine queries, Internet transaction data, consumer behavior, or social media activity. The era of big data has also arrived in higher education as multiple data (e.g., data about multiple student pathways at various types of institutions and data about institutional performance) and technology (e.g., mobile phones, Web sites, applications [apps], social media, and learning management systems)

New Directions for Institutional Research • DOI: 10.1002/ir

become increasingly embedded in the processes that comprise "going to college," such as deciding which college to enroll in, applying for financial aid, enrolling in courses, teaching and learning, interacting with peers and faculty, building community, and providing student services. Soares (2011) argues that all these interactions produce ways for students to "personalize college" (p. 2) by using existing technologies to maneuver college procedures, to learn, and to manage their time and experiences. In addition, he claims, the higher education sector is beginning to see a rise in the data produced from all these interactions that can be used to empower students to make even better choices as their college trajectories continue. Similarly, it is argued that higher education institutions can benefit from using big data to improve decision making, to increase organizational productivity, to highlight an institution's successes and challenges, and to improve student persistence and other outcomes (Dietz-Uhler & Hurn, 2013; Kellen, Recktenwald, & Burr, 2013). Financial and accountability pressures now urge the postsecondary sector to look for solutions to its problems, usually by reallocating funds, by finding savings through automation, or by finding different ways to grow revenue (Kellen et al., 2013). According to Kellen et al. (2013), all these roads lead to big data and analytics and their assumed numerous benefits.

While the notions of *empowerment* and *improved decision making* sound appealing, the reality is that not all students and not all institutions have access to and benefit from these innovations. From my perspective, the discussion of the "personalization" of higher education, cost-effectiveness, efficiency, and the use of big data that emerges from diverse ways to experience and deliver higher education lacks a critical perspective. For that reason, my discussion on the benefits and challenges of big data focuses not only on the usage and exploitation of big data (which, in my opinion, should be done), but also on ways in which big data can be used critically. Furthermore, as stated earlier, initiatives that involve the use of big data (and related technologies) to make higher education more effective and efficient must ground their efforts in a clear understanding of students' (and their families') life circumstances and the ways those circumstances intersect with various institutional contexts (Deil-Amen & Rios-Aguilar, 2014). Big data and technology can play a role in improving access to and success in college, but it is no substitute for solving some of the structural issues that plague the field of higher education (e.g., underfunding of institutions, lack of financial aid to the neediest students, overworked staff and faculty, unequal opportunities to succeed, etc.; Deil-Amen & Rios-Aguilar, 2014). Listed next are some of the benefits of big data that the higher education sector has witnessed in the past 10 years.

Real-Time Data.   Universities often rely on email, listservs, institutional Facebook pages, and traditional surveys as the main communication channels to learn from and to reach out to students. These methods feel cumbersome, slow, irrelevant, and unidirectional in light of many of today's college students' lives. Students seem to have vacated these modes of communication and jumped to texts and other real-time mobile communication tools such as social media platforms (e.g., Instagram, Twitter, LinkedIn, etc.), mobile apps (e.g., Schools App, Campus Quad, PerkEDU, CoachMe, GradGuru, etc.), and learning analytic tools (e.g., Notebowl, Blackboard, E^2Coach, etc.) to help them navigate many facets of their college experiences (e.g., academic, social, family, and work) with greater relevancy and ease. Daily, technological, and educational entrepreneurs are developing new tools to enable prospective and current college students at various institutions to engage in college in a different way and to create interest communities that provide them with the information that is pertinent to students' contexts. While real-time data is now a reality for some students in some institutions, it is not a widespread phenomenon. Furthermore, some of these technologies require students to have Internet connectivity, exposure to the technology, and awareness of the technology's value (Deil-Amen & Rios-Aguilar, 2014). Other technological platforms may require institutions to pay for the services provided through the apps. So, while there is a benefit of producing and using real-time data, there is also the possibility of excluding the experiences of many marginalized students and of thousands of underresourced institutions from these technologies and the opportunities that they afford.

A Window Into Students' College Experiences.   Big (and critical) data and the use of social media and mobile technologies can help college leaders and practitioners get a sense of what all students need to successfully navigate college. For example, in an analysis of about 38,000 community students' posts and comments on a Facebook-based app, Deil-Amen and Rios-Aguilar (2014) found that students used the app most frequently to clarify financial aid disbursement timelines and distribution guidelines. The second most frequent type of comments included students' attempts to clarify income and academic stipulations for qualifying for, maintaining, or losing their financial aid. The students' comments helped some colleges to better understand the areas of weakness and gaps that exist in the financial aid services or programs they provided to students who are in most need. In fact, some colleges started to change the way they responded to students on the app, and, as a consequence, they were able to significantly reduce both the number of inquiries they received on similar issues and the time it took to respond to each inquiry. Now it is important to note that while big data and related technologies can create some small-scale efficiencies, they cannot by themselves change institutional structures, practices, values, and norms (Deil-Amen & Rios-Aguilar, 2014).

Colocation of Services.   The big data era is pushing institutions to change location of the services they deliver to students and the type of data collected from the interaction between students and professionals. More specifically, colleges (including staff, practitioners, and faculty) are now urged to use apps to colocate their services. What this means is that student services (e.g., financial aid and academic and career counseling) can be provided "virtually" as well as in traditional office spaces. Consequently, practitioners are now urged to create *meet-ups* or *hangouts* across campus and/or in specific technological platforms to reach students where they are—home, cafeteria, library, and the like. Similarly, faculty members are encouraged to use technological tools to provide virtual office hours and/or to communicate with students who may not be able to attend these. These colocation strategies are assumed to increase the reach of practitioners, faculty, and staff. However, while using technology to reach out to many students through several virtual means seems an attractive and cost-effective tool, it is important to keep in mind that creating a sophisticated sense of *being there* (as suggested by Hollan and Stornetta in 1992) may not translate into a successful transmission of information or into a meaningful feedback session. In fact, one of the most effective ways to improve college attendance rates is to provide face-to-face support to low-income families when filling out the Free Application for Federal Student Aid (FAFSA). (See Bettinger, Long, Oreopoulos, & Sanbonmatsu [2012] for details on this experiment.) Such evidence appears to somewhat contradict the assumption that technology alone presents a feasible solution to the many issues that colleges face nowadays (e.g., low engagement, low persistence, and completion rates; Deil-Amen & Rios-Aguilar, 2014). In addition, let us not forget that the data generated from these interactions can later be used to evaluate professionals' effectiveness and to measure several aspects of the institution's performance. I elaborate on this point in the next benefit.

Data Analytics, Dashboards, and New Metrics.   Institutions are now able to retrieve real-time analytics on students' needs, interactions, experiences, engagement, outcomes, and much more. Similarly, new ways to integrate, visualize, and examine these data are being suggested to institutions (e.g., data mining, market-based analysis, neural networks and decision trees, graphic and spatial analyses, and text mining and tokenization). The technology sector is presenting (and selling) higher education institutions predetermined "data dashboards" that produce predictive models, metrics, and assessments that, arguably, summarize students' learning, engagement, and interactions with others (e.g., see IBM's [2001] *Analytics for Achievement* framework). I believe the assumption made is that data-driven analytics will allow colleges to deliver a "superior" college experience that will lead to putting students on a trajectory of success. Similarly, institutions assume that the data produced will allow their leaders and staff to make better decisions.

However, the reality is that there are no established best practices about what and how to measure this, and there is no expertise on how to create and/or utilize big data. Furthermore, very few tech entrepreneurs (including app designers) really understand what these metrics mean in the context of students' lives and of existing organizational structures. Most important, lacking from these discussions on analytics and dashboards are critical data that can allow decision makers to unmask inequities and to take a deep and critical look at which experiences and students are being excluded from these various analytics. In short, there is a need to better understand the assumptions behind the metrics being manufactured and utilized and how trends in the development of technology and the production and use of big data are leading to the quantification of the college-going process. As suggested by Espeland and Stevens (2008), we must carefully pay attention to all the dimensions of the process of quantification (i.e., the work it requires, its reactivity, its tendency to discipline human behavior, its polyvalent authority, and its aesthetics), so we can understand both the measurements and their social consequences. Without paying close attention to the quantification of the college-going process, there is the possibility of establishing a new deficit regime that dictates the new guidelines on what to have (or not), what to learn (or not), or how to behave (or not) in order to be successful in college and subsequently.

Challenges of Big Data

In addition to the limitations already discussed, in this section I build upon Boyd and Crawford's (2012) and Manovich's (2011) ideas to elaborate on other aspects of big data that institutional researchers and higher education scholars, practitioners, and leaders must pay attention to.

The Oversimplification of Higher Education.   Although there is hype and money being poured into big data initiatives, there is skepticism about what big data can actually accomplish for the field of higher education (New, 2014). While it is tempting to get seduced by the "Amazonification of higher education" (p. 12), we need to carefully examine whether, for example, student engagement, persistence, and learning are also transactions that can be aggregated and modeled in the same way as we buy products on the Web. The question we need to focus on is how big (and critical) data and their metrics will help us create better tools and services to help all students (particularly those who are more vulnerable) to succeed in school and in life.

Big Data Changes Scholarly Activity.   In addition to changing the capacity to collect and analyze data with unparalleled breadth and depth, big data will profoundly change the way we think about what we know and how we came to know it (Boyd & Crawford, 2012). In other words, big data are changing the type of research we conduct. For that reason, we must ask difficult questions about the algorithms' capacity to predict students' lives, failures, and successes and about the analytics' ability to measure all students' experiences before they crystallize into new deficit paradigms.

Big Data, Metrics, and Their Interpretation.   Big data provide institutional researchers and decision makers with numbers as well as with multiple visuals and graphs. Although these seem objective and irrefutable, we cannot forget that working with data is still subjective. That is, the decisions that determine what will be measured and how the data will be used stem from individuals' interpretations (Boyd & Crawford, 2012). Furthermore, the very basic concept of validity needs also to be reexamined and discussed in this new context. We must not forget that regardless of how big the big data are, how accurate measures are, and how good graphs look, these are all still subject to limitations and biases. The emergence and spread of big data and their analytics require scholars and college leaders to consider the ethical implications of using these data to better serve all students.

Big Data, Meaningful Data?   Just because big data present us with large quantities of data, it does not mean that methodological issues are no longer relevant (Boyd & Crawford, 2012). Understanding sampling, for example, is more important now than ever. Twitter provides a great example of this. Researchers working with tweets often excite audiences stating that they analyzed thousands or millions of tweets. That sounds impressive given that, traditionally, research projects involving sampling techniques have always been labor intensive and very costly. Also, let us not forget that only social scientists working for Google or Facebook will have access to the data that the rest of the scholarly community will not have access to (Manovich, 2011). Still, a large number of tweets, for instance, can be studied, but they are only a sample. Twitter does not represent "all people," and it is an error to assume the terms "people" and "Twitter users" are synonymous: They are a very particular subset (Boyd & Crawford, 2012). Some users have multiple accounts, while some accounts are used by multiple people. Some people never establish an account and simply access Twitter via the Web. Furthermore, Fagioli, Rios-Aguilar, and Deil-Amen (in press) found that the very meanings of the terms "user" and "participation" and "active" need to be critically examined. Actually, one of the most striking findings of their study is that "passive" users of a Facebook-based app are more likely than active users to reenroll in college the subsequent term. Finally, researchers and practitioners need to be careful of examining and interpreting communications over social media as "authentic" (Manovich, 2011). These data are often carefully articulated and systematically managed (Ellison, Heino, & Gibbs, 2006). This does not mean that scholars cannot do interesting research by analyzing larger numbers of tweets, Facebook photos, YouTube videos, and the like—they just have to keep in mind that all these data do not constitute a transparent window into people's imaginations, intentions, motifs, opinions, and ideas (Manovich, 2011).

Big Data and Critical Thinking.   Working with big data has serious methodological and conceptual challenges that are rarely acknowledged by those who embrace the data. Methodologically, we must not forget that merging data is prone to many errors and challenges, even when the process is programmed. Theoretically, we must develop the conceptual tools needed to guide the design of research with big data as well as the interpretation of the results produced by the analyses. As Manovich (2011) clearly articulates, completely automatic analysis of social and cultural data will not produce meaningful results today because the ability of algorithms and metrics to understand the meaning and content of posts, texts, images, video, and other media is still limited. Data cannot be reduced to what can fit in a model or what social graphs can represent (Boyd & Crawford, 2012). Indeed, having the capacity to represent relationships in a graph does not mean that we can now understand how students form and sustain relationships (or networks). The "friendships" displayed on social media sites are not necessarily equivalent to the sociograms that scientists have been studying for decades. Understanding the value and purpose of students' social networks requires deep and careful thinking that goes beyond looking at social graphs. Ideally, we want to combine the human ability to think, understand, and interpret—which algorithms, analytics, and graphs by themselves cannot do—and the ability of computers to analyze massive data in sophisticated ways (Manovich, 2011). Therefore, it is imperative that big data are analyzed rigorously, from diverse theoretical perspectives, and using a variety of methodological approaches. This is the only way that big data will help the higher education community to better serve all students, not only those who happen to access the technology or those whose behavior and experiences are summarized on the data dashboards.

Big Data and New Data Classes.   The availability of big data as well as of software and techniques used to analyze massive volumes of data has brought new possibilities to conduct cutting-edge and meaningful research. However, it requires expertise in many areas, including computer programming, statistics, and data mining techniques. Most of these competencies are not part of the current skill set of institutional researchers and higher education scholars. As a result of the explosion of data and the emergence of computational data analysis as the key scientific and economic approach in contemporary societies, new divisions among professionals are being created (Manovich, 2011). More specifically, Manovich (2011) divides people and organizations into three main categories: those who create data (e.g., users of social media and mobile phones and apps), those who have the means to collect it (e.g., tech entrepreneurs and app designers), and those who have expertise to analyze it (e.g., data scientists with very specific training). Manovich refers to these three groups as "the new 'data-classes' of our big data society" (p. 11). What he does not mention are the "excluded" classes (e.g., those who do not create any data, those who create the data but never benefit from it, and those who do not have expertise to use it and to make sense of it). If the higher education community aspires benefit from the creation and usage of big (and critical) data, then it is imperative that we rethink the training that current and prospective institutional researchers and scholars receive. Furthermore, the higher education community must also consider training "outsiders" (e.g., tech entrepreneurs and app developers) about the meaning of the metrics they create and about the usefulness of the products they design in the context of marginalized students' lives and in the context of the challenges faced by postsecondary institutions. Establishing true collaborative relationships and partnerships in which all these various actors can interact and learn from each other is needed if we aspire to use big (and critical) data to better serve all college students.

Big (and Critical) Data in Higher Education Research

The emergence of social media and related technologies, and the big data that emerge from their use, has created new opportunities to study educational, social, and cultural processes and dynamics in new ways. Indeed, today's college students have embraced social media. These technologies have altered the way students communicate generally and within their college community. Some educational institutions are finding ways to use social media creatively to reach out to students and strengthen their ties to the institution. More than ever, higher education leaders, practitioners, and scholars need to know how to skillfully negotiate these data and technologies to examine, critically, issues of equity in colleges throughout the United States.

In this section, I present a concrete example of how commuter-based community colleges attempt to use social media as a mechanism to increase students' connection to and success in college. I focus my discussion on one particular type of big and critical data—those generated through the use of social media. These data, when combined with other more traditional data sets (e.g., course-level and institutional data) and with interviews, focus groups, and observations, allow institutional researchers, college leaders, and scholars to carefully study issues of equity issues in colleges.

Value and Impact of Social Media in Community Colleges.   With the tremendous increase of community college enrollments and the ubiquitous use of social media such as Facebook, it is critical to examine how community college students incorporate it into their college pursuits, what relationship it has on their college experience, and finally their college success. My co–Principal Investigator (Dr. Regina Deil-Amen) and I have engaged in this important and timely effort. Beginning in fall 2011, as part of a Bill & Melinda Gates Foundation grant-funded intervention, nine urban, small-town, and rural U.S. community colleges (located in Arkansas, Arizona, California, New York, Ohio, Texas, Wisconsin, and Wyoming) were selected to adopt a Facebook-based application, known as the Schools App, for limited use by invited students, staff, faculty, and administrators. (See Table 3.1 for details on the demographic characteristics of selected colleges.)[1] The Schools App is purposefully designed to host, manage, and facilitate social engagement for college students.[2] This app creates a private proprietary community for students attending a specific college, allowing them to make friends, ask questions, share interests, seek advice and information, and get involved by organizing social activities offline. It is crucial to state that the selection of colleges was purposeful. My co-PI and I chose

NEW DIRECTIONS FOR INSTITUTIONAL RESEARCH • DOI: 10.1002/ir

Table 3.1. Characteristics of Participating Community Colleges

| | | | Student Race/Ethnicity | | |
| | | | White (%) | Hispanic (%) | African American (%) |
Institution	Enrollment	Location			
CC #1	15,734	City, Large	6	52	27
CC #2	8,365	City, Small	77	11	2
CC #3	31,250	City, Large	54	4	33
CC #4	13,000	City, Large	33	33	11
CC #5	12,296	Suburban, Large	60	18	4
CC #6	11,783	Suburban, Large	73	3	10
CC #7	28,549	City, Large	38	41	10
CC #8	5,573	Rural, Medium	89	1	2
CC #9	4,905	Rural, Medium	83	7	3

Source: Based on information from IPEDS and the Carnegie Classification, 2010.

colleges that were not considered "privileged," and we chose to focus the analyses on the most vulnerable groups of students at each campus: nontraditional students, returning veterans, racial/ethnic minorities, and low-income students.

This project required the use of big data—actual social media exchanges between community college students and between students and staff (including advisors and faculty)—to understand how community college students use and find meaning in their social media ties in ways that facilitate the exchange of the types of information, social capital, and sense of belonging to academic and professional communities that have been shown to make a difference for educational and occupational advancement, particularly for lower-income and underrepresented minority populations (Fagioli et al., in press). Using big data has enabled my co-PI and I to obtain a more "real-time" sense of with whom these students are communicating (e.g., institutional agents, instructors, peers in class, college peers, family, etc.), what they are communicating about (professional, majors, academic, procedural, personal, financial aid, etc.), and the outcomes (e.g., grade point averages [GPAs] and persistence rates) for those who participate in these online interactions.

In addition to using actual social media exchanges, we needed to combine these with more traditional institutional datasets to assess the impact of usage of social media on students' outcomes. It took us approximately one year to figure out how to assemble our big and critical data. We needed to make sure we could merge the app data that came in various shapes and sizes with institutional data that also vary in content and format. Furthermore, the project required us to learn how to manipulate big data in various ways (e.g., transforming comma separated values [csv] files to friendship matrices) and to navigate different software packages (e.g., moving csv files from Excel to NVivo, UCINET, R, and STATA). Finally, we needed to develop different ways to analyze and visualize the data produced by the app. For example, we have used data mining techniques, social network analyses, econometric analyses, and qualitative analyses to examine patterns in what students are talking about, in their online social ties, and in their academic outcomes (GPA and retention rates). We have created word clouds, sociograms, and maps to help us communicate our findings to several audiences. We continue to examine data generated from about 39,000 community college students who are currently using the app in various ways and from interview data with students and faculty who are users and nonusers of the app.

Additionally, the research project required us to think more deeply about the conceptual frameworks we used to analyze and interpret our data. We knew that existing scholarship (e.g., Kuh, 2001; Tinto, 1993) fails to contemplate the validity and relevance of integration, involvement, engagement, and community for interactions between community college peers in a virtual space (Fagioli et al., in press). Thus, we needed to challenge existing models and utilize new conceptual tools to better understand the dynamics of how connection to college happens for community college students, especially in online environments. For example, we adapted Junco's and Ellison's work on online interactions among college students (see Fagioli et al. [in press] for details on these frameworks) to make sense of community college students' interactions on the Schools App. Besides, we relied on Deil-Amen's (2011) notion of socioacademic integrative moments to examine how these students access the social capital they need to persist in college.

We have also used social network theory (e.g., strength of ties and social capital) to examine the content and meaning of the online ties that community college students are creating in an effort to persist in college. We continue studying how big data and technology are introduced into social contexts using literature on the social construction of technology (SCOT). This scholarship explores social relationships as they are shaped by technology (see Rhoades [1998] on faculty enskilling/deskilling, and relations with administration) as well as differences between the interests of designers and users of new technologies. It might seem counterintuitive that big data and social media are presented as solutions to problems embedded in limited human interactions of students with faculty, other professionals, and peers. Yet in a high-tech, knowledge society filled with the explosion of new communication technologies and user-generated social media that lends more control to the student, it makes sense to use these. Indeed, the policy discourse in higher education reveals regular invocation of high-tech solutions to learning and productivity challenges in higher education. However, as discussed earlier, big data are not the panacea for higher education's problems.

What we have learned so far from our research is that there is a relationship between using the app and students' outcomes. In fact, both

NEW DIRECTIONS FOR INSTITUTIONAL RESEARCH • DOI: 10.1002/ir

"active" and "passive" users across all colleges were significantly more likely to reenroll in college (12% and 27% respectively) compared to nonmembers (see Fagioli et al. [in press] for details on these findings). Keep in mind that most app users in our sample are considered vulnerable students (i.e., 41% are nontraditional students, 45% are considered racial/ethnic minority students, 56% receive financial aid, and 31% are enrolled in at least one remedial course). Furthermore, we have found that the app functions as a "virtual window" for colleges that exposes students' need for procedural college-going knowledge. However, they do possess initiative to communicate and network to acquire what they lack to navigate highly complex institutions and processes. Students also possess a desire for an emotionally supportive, information-sharing, helpful community and a willingness to create it (see Deil-Amen & Rios-Aguilar [2014] for details on these findings). It is important to keep in mind that the impact of the app was restricted by gaps in students' exposure to it, by students' awareness of its value, and by sporadic engagement.

Implications of Using Big Data for Critical Quantitative Research in Higher Education

Without a doubt, the big data revolution is here. It is argued by some organizations, such as the Western Interstate Commission on Higher Education (WICHE; New, 2014), that by using big data to improve instruction, match students to programs and employment, make education financing more transparent, and increase the efficiency of system administrations, the education sector could see an increase of $900 billion to $1.2 trillion in additional annual value (New, 2014). However, as I discussed in this chapter, the alleged benefits of big data in higher education are not automatic and will not be distributed evenly. Furthermore, if data are not used from a critical perspective, we will end up simply finding a sophisticated way to reproduce inequities. For that reason, I propose that the higher education community focuses on designing, producing, and using *big and critical data* to provide equal educational opportunities to all students. This effort will require a different type of training for institutional researchers, leaders, scholars, and practitioners. At the same time, it necessitates the involvement of marginalized students, families, and communities to inform our studies, metrics, and interpretation of results. Failing to understand how big data (and its related technologies) intersect with educational opportunity will perpetuate the idea that only certain students and institutions are valuable and worthy of our investments, thus perpetuating inequities.

Notes

1. For more information on the Getting Connected research project, go to http://gettingconnectedresearch.com
2. For more information on the Schools App, go to http://www.uversity.com

New Directions for Institutional Research • DOI: 10.1002/ir

References

Bettinger, E., Long, B., Oreopoulos, P., & Sanbonmatsu, L. (2012). The role of application assistance and information in college decisions: Results from the H&R Block FAFSA experiment. *The Quarterly Journal of Economics, 127*(3), 1205–1242.

The big data conundrum: How to define it? (2013, October). *MIT Technology Review*. Retrieved from http://www.technologyreview.com/view/519851/the-big-data -conundrum-how-to-define-it

Boyd, D., & Crawford, K. (2012). Critical questions for big data: Provocations for a cultural, technological, and scholarly phenomenon. *Information, Communication & Society, 15*(5), 662–679.

Deil-Amen, R. (2011). Socio-academic integrative moments: Rethinking academic and social integration among two-year college students in career-oriented programs. *Journal of Higher Education, 82*(1), 54–91.

Deil-Amen, R., & Rios-Aguilar, C. (2014). From FAFSA to Facebook: The role of technology in navigating the financial aid process. In A. Kelly & S. Goldrick-Rab (Eds.), *Reinventing financial aid: Charting a new course to college affordability* (pp. 75–100). Harvard Education Press.

Dietz-Uhler, B., & Hurn, J. (2013). Using learning analytics to predict (and improve) student success: A faculty perspective. *Journal of Interactive Online Learning, 12*(1), 17–26.

Ellison, N., Heino, R., & Gibbs, J. (2006). Managing impressions online: Self-presentation process in the online dating environment. *Journal of Computer Mediated Communication, 11*(2), 415–441. doi:10.1111/j.1083-6101.2006.00020.x

Espeland, W., & Stevens, M. (2008). A sociology of quantification. *European Journal of Sociology, 49*, 401–436.

Executive Office of the President. (2014). Big data: Seizing opportunities, preserving values. Retrieved from http://www.scribd.com/doc/221447085/White-House -Big-Data-Privacy-Report

Fagioli, L., Rios-Aguilar, C., & Deil-Amen, R. (in press). Changing the context of engagement: Using Facebook to increase community college students' persistence and success. *Teachers College Record*.

Hollan, J., & Stornetta, S. (1992). Beyond being there. In P. Bauersfeld, J. Bennett, & G. Lynch (Eds.), *CHI'92 proceedings of the SIGCHI conference on human factors in computing systems* (pp. 119–125). New York, NY: ACM Press. doi:10.1145/142750.142769

IBM. (2001). *Analytics for achievement: Understand success and boost performance in primary and secondary education*. White paper. Retrieved from http://public.dhe .ibm.com/common/ssi/ecm/en/ytw03149caen/YTW03149CAEN.PDF

Kellen, V., Recktenwald, A., & Burr, S. (2013). *Applying big data to higher education: A case study* (Data Insight and Social BI, Executive Report, 8[13]). Arlington, MA: Cutter Consortium.

Kuh, G. D. (2001). Assessing what really matters to student learning: Inside the National Survey of Student Engagement. *Change, 33*(3), 10–17, 66.

Manovich, L. (2011). Trending: The promises and the challenges of big social data. In M. K. Gold (Ed.), *Debates in the digital humanities*. Minneapolis, MN: University of Minnesota Press. Retrieved from http://manovich.net/content/04-projects/066 -trending-the-promises-and-the-challenges-of-big-social-data/64-article-2011.pdf

National Science Foundation (NSF). (2012). *Solicitation 12-499: Core techniques and technologies for advancing big data science & engineering (BIGDATA), 2012*. Retrieved from http://www.nsf.gov/pubs/2012/nsf12499/nsf12499.pdf

New, J. (2014, February). Higher education's big (data) bang. *eCampus News*. Retrieved from http://jakenewdotcom.files.wordpress.com/2014/03/pages3.pdf

Rhoades, G. (1998). The production politics of teaching and technology: Deskilling, enskilling, and managerial extension. In *Managed professionals: Unionized faculty and restructuring academic labor* (pp. 173–210). Albany, NY: State University of New York Press.

Soares, L. (2011). *The personalization of higher education: Using technology to enhance the college experience.* Washington, DC: Center for American Progress.

Stage, F. K., & Wells, R. S. (2014). Critical quantitative inquiry in context. In F. K. Stage & R. S. Wells (Eds.), *New Directions for Institutional Research: No. 158. New scholarship in critical quantitative research—Part 1: Studying institutions and people in context* (pp. 1–7). San Francisco, CA: Jossey-Bass.

Tinto, V. (1993). *Leaving college: Rethinking the causes and cures of student attrition* (2nd. ed.). Chicago, IL: University of Chicago Press.

Ward, J., & Barker, A. (2013). *Undefined by data: A survey of big data definitions.* Technical Report. Fife, UK: School of Computer Science, University of St. Andrews.

CECILIA RIOS-AGUILAR *is an associate professor of education at the School of Educational Studies at Claremont Graduate University.*

This chapter discusses the utility of person-centered approaches to critical quantitative researchers. These techniques, which identify groups of individuals who share similar attributes, experiences, or outcomes, are contrasted with more commonly used variable-centered approaches. An illustrative example of a latent class analysis of the college financing strategies of a nationally representative sample of science, technology, engineering, and mathematics bachelor's degree holders is presented.

4

Application of Person-Centered Approaches to Critical Quantitative Research: Exploring Inequities in College Financing Strategies

Lindsey Malcom-Piqueux

Critical quantitative researchers aim to uncover the existence of systematic inequities in educational processes and outcomes through analysis of quantitative data (Stage, 2007). Critical quantitative research also involves questioning the models, measures, and methods typically used in conventional quantitative approaches and employing those better capable of describing the experiences of historically understudied and marginalized groups (Stage, 2007). This chapter discusses the utility of person-centered approaches to doing critical quantitative research that address questions related to educational equity.

Person-centered approaches are concerned with identifying groups of individuals that are qualitatively different from one another but share similar attributes, experiences, or outcomes with those individuals in the same category. These approaches, which are underutilized in the higher education research literature, are particularly useful for revealing educational inequities that might otherwise go unnoticed using more common variable-centered approaches.

In this chapter, I describe person-centered approaches and contrast them with more common variable-centered approaches. I then discuss the ways in which person-centered approaches can be used in critical quantitative work to explore questions related to equity for historically

NEW DIRECTIONS FOR INSTITUTIONAL RESEARCH, no. 163 © 2015 Wiley Periodicals, Inc.
Published online in Wiley Online Library (wileyonlinelibrary.com) • DOI: 10.1002/ir.20086

disadvantaged groups. The chapter concludes with a brief illustrative example of a critical, person-centered analysis of students' college financing strategies.

Understanding Person-Centered Approaches

Across a range of disciplines, person-centered approaches to analyzing quantitative data increasingly have been used to study the development and experiences of individuals. In contrast to the more commonly used variable-centered approaches that aim to explore associations among variables, person-centered approaches seek to characterize differences across groups of individuals (Jung & Wickrama, 2008; Masyn, 2013; Muthén & Muthén, 2000; Samuelsen & Dayton, 2010). Thus, although variable-centered approaches are ideal for understanding the impact of a particular variable on an outcome of interest, person-centered approaches are appropriate when a researcher wishes to identify a group of individuals that function in a similar way or have shared a set of attributes or experiences (Jung & Wickrama, 2008; Muthén & Muthén, 2000).

Discriminant analysis, cluster analysis, and mixture modeling are examples of person-centered approaches that can be applied to group individuals into categories, each one of which contains individuals who are similar to each other and qualitatively different from individuals in other categories (Muthén & Muthén, 2000). Latent class analysis (LCA), latent profile analysis (LPA), and latent class growth analysis (LCGA) are special cases of mixture modeling (McLachlan & Peel, 2000). In the case of cluster analysis, discriminant analysis, LCA, and LPA, categories represent specific typologies or experiences; in LCGA, categories represent specific developmental trajectories, that is, change in typology or experiences over time.

Researchers select the appropriate person-centered approach based on their research questions and the nature of the data they wish to analyze. Discriminant analysis requires that group membership is known from the data (Huberty, 2005), whereas group membership is not known a priori (i.e., it is unobserved) in cluster analysis, LCA, LPA, and LCGA. Instead, these methods are based on the assumption that the observed or manifest variables are associated because of an underlying, unobserved construct, and they seek to group similar individuals on that unobserved construct. This latent, or unobserved, construct is the antecedent to the manifest, or observed, variables (Goodman, 2002).

Traditional cluster analysis is a non-model-based technique that uses categorical and continuous variables to determine group membership for individuals in the data (Pastor, 2010). LCA, LPA, and LCGA are all model-based techniques used to determine the probability of group membership (Muthén & Muthén, 2000; Samuelsen & Dayton, 2010); however, they employ different types of data. LCA uses cross-sectional categorical data (i.e., dichotomous, ordered-category, nominal), while cross-sectional, continuous data are suitable for LPA. Categorical and continuous cross-sectional data can be analyzed together in a more general finite mixture model. LCGA analyzes longitudinal data to group individuals into latent trajectory classes (Muthén & Muthén, 2000).

Person-centered approaches require the researcher to characterize the groups identified in the analysis by qualitatively interpreting the item probability or response patterns of each class or profile. Person-centered approaches can also be integrated with variable-centered approaches to explore the determinants of class membership (e.g., race, gender, socioeconomic status) or to examine the relationship between class membership and outcome variables (Masyn, 2013; Muthén & Muthén, 2000).

Use of Person-Centered Approaches in Higher Education Research

Person-centered approaches have been used across the health, medical, and social science research literature for quite some time; however, their use in the field of higher education is quite limited (Denson & Ing, 2014). With few exceptions, quantitative work in the higher education research literature has employed variable-centered methodological approaches to describe the relationships among independent and dependent variables and to predict outcomes. Though a few relatively recent studies employ LCA and/or LPA (e.g., Denson & Ing, 2014; Pastor, Barron, Miller, & Davis, 2007; Weerts, Cabrera, & Mejias, 2013), applications of these and other person-centered analytical techniques are largely absent from the higher education research literature.

Denson and Ing (2014) argue for increased use of LCA in higher education research, citing the power of the methodological approach to group college students into classes or typologies for a range of psychosocial constructs central to student learning and development. They also present a thoroughly explained example of LCA focusing on the concept of pluralistic orientation, defined as "an indicator of one's ability to work effectively with others of diverse backgrounds, being open to new ideas and different perspectives, and being empathetic with other perspectives" (p. 511). In their analysis of data from the UCLA Cooperative Institutional Research Program (CIRP) Freshman Survey, Denson and Ing selected survey items that were relevant to the concept of pluralistic orientation using theory and higher education research literature as a guide. They then conducted a latent class analysis and identified four classes, or groups, of students with similar patterns of responses on the observed survey items related to pluralistic orientation. These four classes were qualitatively different from one another. Based on the survey item response patterns associated with each of the four classes, Denson and Ing interpreted the groups to represent students with (1) high pluralistic orientation; (2) high disposition, low skill (i.e., possessed tolerance for difference but lacked the ability to negotiate differences); (3) low disposition, high skill (i.e., lacked tolerance for difference but possessed ability to negotiate difference); and (4) low pluralistic orientation. Denson and Ing also used a variable-centered approach (i.e., multinomial logistic regression) to explore the extent to which race, gender, and socioeconomic status were associated with class membership.

Why Use Person-Centered Approaches in Critical Quantitative Research?

Person-centered approaches are particularly well suited to conducting critical quantitative research due to their ability to identify groups of students who have qualitatively different college experiences and outcomes. At present, most critical quantitative research studies that aim to explore racial, ethnic, and class-based inequities in educational processes and outcomes tend to characterize (1) the association between the dimension of identity of interest (e.g., race/ethnicity, socioeconomic status) and one or more outcomes (e.g., persistence, completion); or (2) the way in which identity variables like race, gender, and class moderate the relationships among student experiences, institutional characteristics, and outcomes using descriptive or multivariate techniques.

Given the growing emphasis on the ways in which multiple dimensions of identity intersect to structure college access, experiences, and outcomes, and the goals of critical quantitative inquiry, person-centered approaches are a powerful methodological tool in the arsenal of quantitative criticalists. As discussed, person-centered approaches are capable of (1) identifying classes (i.e., groups of individuals that share similar attributes and experiences); and (2) determining whether these experiences are systematically structured by race, ethnicity, gender, class, and the like. In other words, person-centered approaches can be used to reveal inequities in a manner that is distinct from variable-centered approaches.

For example, consider a data set that includes measures of student involvement, perceptions of campus climate for diversity, and student background characteristics. While a variable-centered approach (e.g., regression) might be used to characterize the relationships among race, students' perceptions of campus climate, and their levels of involvement, a person-centered approach (e.g., latent profile analysis) could be used to differentiate between groups of students with distinct patterns of responses on the variables related to involvement and perceptions of campus climate for diversity. There might be a subset of respondents who report low levels of involvement, but one portion of these less involved students perceives a negative climate for diversity, while the other has neutral feelings about the campus climate for diversity. Person-centered approaches are capable of distinguishing these heterogeneous groups. The group of students reporting low levels of involvement and negative perceptions of campus climate for diversity are experiencing college in a way that is very distinct from the second group of students who are also less involved but do not perceive campus climate as an issue for them.

Person-centered approaches are also appropriate for doing critical quantitative work because of their relevance to educational practice. In addition to revealing inequities in educational processes, experiences, and outcomes, critical quantitative research seeks to inform policy and guide action to redress these inequities (Stage, 2007; Stage & Wells, 2014). Person-centered approaches can be used to identify groups of students with shared attributes that can then be targeted for appropriate interventions to facilitate their development and achievement of desired outcomes (Denson & Ing, 2014). Returning to the earlier example on student involvement and campus climate, the group of less involved students with negative perceptions of the climate for diversity might benefit from institutional efforts to create a more inclusive and positive climate for diversity, while the second group of less involved students might face different types of barriers to student involvement.

In sum, person-centered approaches are appropriate for critical quantitative inquiry due to their ability to characterize student experiences in a holistic manner and uncover inequities in educational experiences and outcomes, and to their relevance to practice. To better illustrate how person-centered approaches can be applied, I now present a critical quantitative exploration of students' college financing strategies using latent class analysis. Before discussing the study's goals, methods, and findings, I contextualize the example with a brief review of the literature.

Using LCA to Examine Racial/Ethnic Differences in College Financing Strategies

Rising college costs coupled with stagnant need-based grant aid and an increased reliance on student loans contribute to ongoing race, ethnicity, and class-based inequities in higher education access and outcomes in complex ways. Previous research has illustrated that populations historically underrepresented in higher education (i.e., students of color, first-generation students, and low-income students) are more susceptible to "sticker shock" and have differing perceptions of college affordability and financial aid (e.g., Heller, 1997; McDonough & Calderone, 2006; St. John, 2006). While considerations of college costs influence the college choice process for nearly all students, concerns about affordability play a significant role in the decision-making process for historically underrepresented students, sometimes leading them to attend less expensive (and often less selective) institutions, in spite of available financial aid (Long, 2008; St. John, 2006).

Current data also reveal that historically disadvantaged students rely more heavily on financial aid in general, and loans in particular (College Board, 2013). Lower-income students attending four-year institutions are more likely to borrow than students from wealthier families and complete college with higher debt levels than their high-income counterparts (College Board, 2013). In terms of racial disparities, Black college students borrow at higher rates and amass significantly higher debt burdens than White, Asian, and Latino students (Aud, Fox, & KewalRamani, 2010). These disparate borrowing rates may contribute to inequities in educational outcomes, as there is some evidence that loans are not as effective in promoting persistence as grant aid (e.g., Alon, 2007) and that borrowing and higher debt levels are negatively associated with degree completion (e.g., Kim, 2007) and graduate school enrollment (e.g., Malcom & Dowd, 2012). Further, as student loan debt has implications for future disposable income, creditworthiness, and savings, these differences in the ways in which students finance college also have the potential to contribute to future inequities in wealth (Goldrick-Rab, Kelchen, & Houle, 2014; Price, 2004).

Because the ways in which students pay for college can exacerbate existing educational and economic inequities, research on the usage and effects of financial aid ought to employ critical quantitative approaches. Critical quantitative research aims to uncover inequities experienced along race, class, gender, and other dimensions of identity (Stage, 2007; Stage & Wells, 2014). Quantitative criticalists also seek to identify whether and how policy perpetuates systematic inequities (Stage & Wells, 2014). Indeed, a great deal of the financial aid research literature focuses on identifying racial, ethnic, and socioeconomic differences in the use of financial aid and its effects on educational, economic, and workforce outcomes. Numerous scholars have explored the prevalence at which various populations of students use specific forms of financial aid, their attitudes toward these forms of aid, and the effects of financial aid on student outcomes like persistence, completion, and graduate school attendance. Their empirical work has informed critiques of current financial aid policy and the ways in which these policies further inequity.

Purpose of the Study.   As discussed earlier, much of the previous research on financial aid explores differences in the usage and effects of financial aid along various dimensions of identity. Although these studies are highly informative and serve as the basis of our current understanding of how students pay for college, the variable-centered methodological approaches typically used are unable to identify students' college financing strategies—that is, the qualitatively different ways in which students (and their families) use multiple forms and sources of financial support in combination with one another to pay for college. For this task, person-centered quantitative approaches are necessary. The purpose of the current study is to (1) identify the college financing strategies used by a national sample of college graduates; and (2) examine the patterns of college financing strategies by race/ethnicity.

Data.   To accomplish the listed aims, I analyzed data from the National Science Foundation's National Survey of Recent College Graduates (NSRCG).[1,2] The NSRCG is administered approximately every two years to a nationally representative sample of individuals who have earned either a bachelor's or master's degree in the two academic years preceding the survey reference date. The 2003 NSRCG, which is used in this analysis, provides information on individuals ($N = 10,381$) who earned a bachelor's or master's degree in science, technology, engineering, or mathematics (STEM) from a U.S. institution between July 1, 2000, and June 30, 2002. I limited the analytical sample to individuals who earned a STEM bachelor's degree during this period ($N_{\text{analytical}} = 7,700$), as these students completed college within the same financial aid policy context. Though these data are somewhat dated, NSF discontinued the collection of financial aid data on the NSRCG after 2006. Therefore, the 2003 NSRCG provides some of the most recent financial aid data available from a nationally representative sample of STEM bachelor's degree holders.

Individuals in the 2003 NSRCG sample responded to survey items regarding their educational experiences and aspirations, employment situation, work-related experiences, and demographic background. The NSRCG includes eight financial aid variables that represent a specific form of financial aid/support: (1) loans from a school, bank, or government; (2) work study; (3) scholarships/grants; (4) earnings; (5) employer support; (6) parental/familial support not to be repaid; (7) parental/familial loan; and (8) any other source. These eight variables were mutually exclusive and dichotomous, with a response of "1" indicating that the respondent received financial aid/support through the specified mechanism and "0" indicating that no support was received through the specified mechanism. Other NSRCG variables also relevant to this analysis include respondents' race and ethnicity, parental education levels, and the control of respondents' baccalaureate-granting institution.

Method.   In order to characterize the underlying financing strategies indicated by the patterns of use of the eight forms of financial support, I conducted a latent class analysis to group STEM bachelor's degree recipients into different types, or classes, of financing strategies. As described earlier, LCA is an analytical technique that aims to uncover clusters of individuals who are similar with respect to a set of characteristics measured by categorical outcomes (Andersen, 1994; Goodman, 2002; McCutcheon, 2002). For the purposes of this application, the measured characteristics correspond to the observed, or manifest, responses indicating the eight forms of financial support. My application of latent class analysis is based on the assumption that the observed financial aid indicator variables are associated because of an underlying, unobserved factor (i.e., the financing strategy). For example, an individual whose strategy is to finance college while avoiding debt will have a different pattern of responses on the eight financial support indicator variables than someone who seeks out financial aid from any source, including loans. This assumption is illustrated in Figure 4.1. It follows then that the relationship between any two manifest financial support indicator variables can be accounted for by the latent variable, college financing strategy

Figure 4.1. College Financing Strategy Precedes Financial Aid Indicator Variables

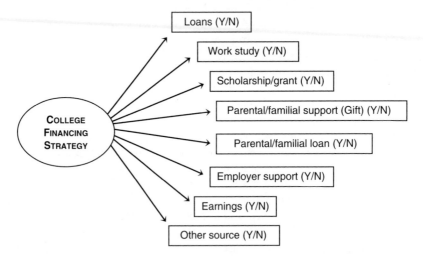

(McCutcheon, 2002). A consequence of this assumption is that individuals whose response patterns on the NSRCG questions regarding financial support resembled one another had a similar underlying college financing strategy.

As stated, there are eight dichotomous financial aid indicator variables and 256 (2^8) possible response patterns. Presumably, each possible response pattern observed in the data could represent a latent class; however, the probabilistic parameterization of the latent class model assumes that measurement error could cause some of the responses observed in the data to be the result of misclassification. Thus, the observed distribution of responses could be due to a smaller number of classes. In latent class analysis, the researcher is able to specify the number of latent classes used to fit the data, and the resulting model can be tested to determine if it is an adequate representation of the observed data. Fit statistics are used to determine the number of classes of the best-fitting solution.

For each financial aid indicator variable, the conditional probability of using that form of financial support is reported for each latent class. I graphed these conditional probabilities and formulated qualitative interpretations for the classes. Additionally, the LCA derived probabilities of class membership for each respondent in the NSRCG data set. I assumed that each respondent was a member of the class for which he or she had the highest probability of membership. I then conducted cross-tabulations of the class membership by race/ethnicity for subsamples of interest, in order to assess the association between college financing strategy and race/ethnicity.

Findings. Based on comparison of model-fit indices from two-, three-, and four-class solutions, a three-latent-class model was selected.

Table 4.1. Conditional Probabilities of Using Forms of Financial Aid, by Latent Class

Form of Financial Aid	Latent Class		
	Class 1 (%)	Class 2 (%)	Class 3 (%)
Work study	2.1	3.3	48.4
Loans (from school, bank, or government)	60.9	26.2	84.5
Earnings	53.2	47.2	67.9
Employer support	23.5	2.3	6.2
Scholarships/grants	45.6	44.9	87.2
Parental/familial support (not to be repaid)	14.9	100.0	63.2
Parental/familial loan	6.4	8.4	9.7
Other source	5.8	1.1	1.0

Source: Analyses of the NSF 2003 National Survey of Recent College Graduates.

These three latent classes represent the three financing strategies employed by students in the sample and were labeled (1) self-support, (2) parental support, and (3) distributed support.

These three latent classes structure the NSRCG response cases with respect to the set of financial aid indicator variables. The conditional probabilities of using each of the eight forms of financial aid for each of the three classes are shown in Table 4.1 and graphed in Figure 4.2.

Figure 4.2. Financial Aid Support Mechanism Probability Profiles

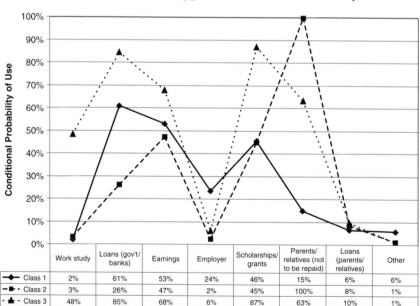

Based on the patterns of conditional probabilities of using a particular form of financial aid, I interpreted the latent classes to represent three distinct college financing strategies: Members of Class 1 financed college by being "self-supporters"—that is, they received little to no parental support, instead relying primarily on loans, earnings, employer support, and scholarships/grants. Members of Class 2 can be described as being "parentally supported"—that is, they had a high probability of receiving parental/familial support not to be repaid and mid-to-low probabilities of using loans, earnings, and scholarships/grants. Member of the final class, Class 3, financed college through "distributed support"—that is, they had a high probability of using multiple forms of financial aid ranging from loans, work study, earnings, scholarships/grants, and parental/familial support (not to be repaid). My qualitative interpretations are summarized in Table 4.2.

For each respondent in the data set, conditional probabilities of belonging to each of the aforementioned latent classes were calculated based on his or her responses on the eight financial aid indicator variables. Each respondent was assigned to the class for which he or she had the highest probability of membership. Based on these class assignments, 16.2% of all respondents employed a self-support college financing strategy, 35.4% of respondents used a parental-support financing strategy, and the remaining 48.4% of respondents used a distributed support financing strategy. Using descriptive statistics, I was also able to examine the racial/ethnic differences in the college financing strategies employed by STEM baccalaureates. I explore the results for racial/ethnic differences in college financing strategies in public and private institutions separately due to the differences in cost and in the availability of institutional grant aid across these two institutional types.

Table 4.2. Summary and Interpretation of Latent Classes

Self-Support	Parental Support	Distributed Support
Primarily relied on Loans	**Primarily relied on** Parental/familial gifts (not to be repaid)	**Primarily relied on** Loans
Earnings Employer support	Earnings Scholarships/grants	Earnings Scholarships/grants Work study
To a lesser extent Scholarships/grants	**To a lesser extent** Loans	**To a lesser extent** Parental/familial gifts (not to be repaid)
Little to no Work study Parental/familial gifts (not to be repaid)	**Little to no** Work study Employer support	**Little to no** Employer support

New Directions for Institutional Research • DOI: 10.1002/ir

Table 4.3. Racial/Ethnic Differences in College Financing Strategies of STEM Bachelor's Degree Recipients From Public Colleges/Universities

		Race/Ethnicity				
College Financing Strategy		Asian (%)	Black (%)	Latino (%)	White (%)	Total (%)
Uncorrected	Self-support	13.9	20.3	21.6	18.2	17.6
$\chi^2 = 181.7570\ df = 8$						
	Parental support	46.5	18.5	29.8	40.5	38.9
Design-based						
$F(6.59, 1409.70) =$	Distributed support	39.7	61.2	48.6	41.2	43.5
$12.1554, p < 0.001$						

Source: Analyses of NSF 2003 *National Survey of Recent College Graduates* (NSRCG), using final survey weight (WTSURVY).
Notes: Column proportions may not sum to total due to rounding.
Design-based *F* statistics are presented to account for the complex sample design of the 2003 NSRCG.

Among STEM bachelor's degree recipients from public four-year colleges and universities, Latinos and Blacks were most likely to employ self-supporting college financing strategies, compared to Asians and Whites. As shown in Table 4.3, more than 20% of Blacks and Latinos employed self-supporting financing strategy, compared to 18% of Whites and nearly 14% of Asian STEM graduates. Asians and Whites were most likely to draw on parental support to pay for college, compared to just 18.5% of Blacks and just below 30% of Latino students who employed this financing strategy. Black STEM degree graduates from public four-year institutions were most likely to employ a distributed-support strategy (i.e., one that draws on multiple forms of financial aid), with Latinos the second most likely to enact this strategy.

Table 4.4 illustrates racial/ethnic differences in college financing strategies among STEM bachelor's degree recipients at private, nonprofit colleges and universities. Perhaps due to the higher average tuition levels at private four-year institutions, fewer students of all racial/ethnic backgrounds employed a self-support financing strategy; nevertheless, Blacks and Latinos were more likely to be self-supporters than Asian and White students. Asian and White students employed the parental-support strategy at greater rates than their Black and Latino counterparts, while Black and Latino students were most likely to use a distributed-support strategy.

In order to understand whether these racial/ethnic differences in college financing strategies were attributable to the disproportionate rates at which Blacks and Latinos come from lower socioeconomic backgrounds, I conducted cross-tabulations of the college financing strategies by race/ethnicity for students whose parents are college graduates. Although parental education is an imperfect proxy for SES, the results are informative. Table 4.5 illustrates that even among STEM bachelor's degree

Table 4.4. Racial/Ethnic Differences in College Financing Strategies of STEM Bachelor's Degree Recipients From Private, Not-for-Profit Colleges/Universities

		Race/Ethnicity				
College Financing Strategy		Asian (%)	Black (%)	Latino (%)	White (%)	Total (%)
Uncorrected $\chi^2 = 100.4644$ $df = 8$	Self-support	6.6	16.7	13.5	12.8	12.8
	Parental support	34.0	14.6	23.4	31.2	30.0
Design-based $F(6.53, 1397.99) = 4.0768, p < 0.001$	Distributed support	59.4	68.7	63.2	56.0	57.2

Source: Analyses of NSF 2003 *National Survey of Recent College Graduates* (NSRCG), using final survey weight (WTSURVY).
Notes: Column proportions may not sum to total due to rounding.
Design-based *F* statistics are presented to account for the complex sample design of the 2003 NSRCG.

recipients whose parents completed at least a bachelor's degree, racial/ethnic differences in college financing strategies persist. In particular, Blacks whose parents completed a bachelor's degree or higher are more likely than similarly situated Asians, Whites, and Latinos to finance college using the self-support strategy or the distributed-support strategy and are less likely than all other groups to use a parental-support strategy.

Discussion.   This analysis suggests that there are systematic racial/ethnic differences in the college financing strategies of STEM bachelor's degree recipients, with Blacks and Latinos more likely than Whites and Asians to employ self-support and distributed-support strategies to finance college. Blacks and Latinos are also less likely to use a parental-support strategy.

Table 4.5. Racial/Ethnic Differences in College Financing Strategies of Non-First-Generation STEM Bachelor's Degree Recipients

		Race/Ethnicity				
College Financing Strategy		Asian (%)	Black (%)	Latino (%)	White (%)	Total (%)
Uncorrected $\chi^2 = 96.6712$ $df = 8$	Self-support	9.3	16.0	11.5	11.5	11.5
	Parental support	53.1	25.9	42.3	44.8	44.9
Design-based $F(6.35, 1359.53) = 5.0234, p < 0.001$	Distributed support	37.6	58.2	46.2	43.8	43.6

Source: Analyses of NSF 2003 *National Survey of Recent College Graduates* (NSRCG), using final survey weight (WTSURVY).
Notes: Column proportions may not sum to total due to rounding.
Design-based *F* statistics are presented to account for the complex sample design of the 2003 NSRCG.

While some of these racial/ethnic differences in college financing strategies may be attributable to socioeconomic status, the disparate rates at which Blacks relied on self-support and distributed-support strategies compared to Whites, Asians, and Latinos remained among students whose parents attained a bachelor's degree. These findings, while not conclusive, suggest that Blacks may be experiencing systematic race-based inequities.

These findings are aligned with prior research on racial/ethnic differences in the reliance on and use of financial aid. However, while previous work has focused on the pattern with which racial minorities and low-income students use individual forms of financial aid with variable-centered approaches, the current study uses latent class analysis, a person-centered approach, to characterize the underlying financing strategy. This person-centered analysis provides a better understanding of how different groups use family resources and financial aid in combination with one another to pay for college in qualitatively different ways. Rather than simply determining that one demographic group borrows more or receives grants more prevalently than other groups, as previous variable-centered studies have shown, this study reveals that there are fundamental differences in the approach that students take to pay for college and that these differences are structured by race and ethnicity.

Because of the differential ways financial aid affects current and future educational and economic outcomes, the differences in college financing strategies revealed in this critical quantitative analysis have the potential to exacerbate existing inequities in educational and economic attainment. Although additional research is needed to better understand the complex mechanisms that drive the racial/ethnic differences in college financing strategies revealed in this analysis, the current study can inform future critical quantitative research on financial aid.

Conclusion

This chapter describes the utility of person-centered approaches in critical quantitative inquiry. Though these methods have not been widely used in higher education research, they have potential to reveal inequities in the experiences and outcomes of different populations of college students. In the chapter, I present an application of latent class analysis to the study of financial aid that (1) identifies the underlying strategies students employ to pay for college and (2) reveals key differences in these strategies by race and ethnicity. The next steps of this analysis would be to integrate LCA with appropriate variable-centered approaches (i.e., multinomial logistic regression) to better characterize the determinants of students' college financing strategies. Regression analyses can also be used in concert with LCA to understand the relationship between college financing strategies and postbaccalaureate educational and labor market outcomes (e.g., graduate school attendance, employment sector). Person-centered approaches can also be used by institutional researchers to identify groups of students who employ different strategies to pay for college and to target for intervention those who may rely on college financing strategies that may have detrimental effects on outcomes, such as persistence and degree completion (e.g., offering additional or more desirable forms of aid).

Critical quantitative research challenges scholars of higher education and institutional researchers to pose critical questions about equity (Stage, 2007; Stage & Wells, 2014) and to use their findings to guide action aimed at bringing about change (Baez, 2007; Stage & Wells, 2014). Person-centered methodological approaches have great potential for meeting these challenges.

Notes

1. The use of NSF data does not imply NSF endorsement of research methods or conclusions contained in this chapter.

2. The results presented are drawn from a larger study of STEM bachelor's degree recipients and their institutional and financial aid pathways. While other data sets—for example, the National Postsecondary Student Aid Survey (NPSAS)—include more detailed information on students' use of financial aid, the NSRCG was used as it surveys a nationally representative sample of STEM undergraduate degree holders.

References

Alon, S. (2007). The influence of financial aid in leveling group differences in graduating from elite institutions. *Economics of Education Review*, 26(3), 296–311.

Andersen, E. B. (1994). *The statistical analysis of categorical data* (3rd ed.). Berlin: Springer-Verlag.

Aud, S., Fox, M., & KewalRamani, A. (2010). *Status and trends in the education of racial and ethnic groups* (NCES 2010-015). Washington, DC: National Center for Education Statistics, U.S. Department of Education.

Baez, B. (2007). Thinking critically about the "critical": Quantitative research as social critique. In F. K. Stage (Ed.), *New Directions for Institutional Research: No. 133. Using quantitative data to answer critical questions* (pp. 17–23). San Francisco, CA: Jossey-Bass.

College Board. (2013). *Trends in student aid: 2013*. New York, NY: Author.

Denson, N., & Ing, M. (2014). Latent class analysis in higher education: An illustrative example of pluralistic orientation. *Research in Higher Education*, 55, 508–526. doi:10.1007/s11162-013-9324-5

Goldrick-Rab, S., Kelchen, R., & Houle, J. (2014). *The color of student debt: Implications for federal loan program reforms for Black students and historically black colleges and universities*. Madison, WI: The Hope Lab, University of Wisconsin-Madison.

Goodman, L. A. (2002). Latent class analysis: The empirical study of latent types, latent variables, and latent structures. In J. A. Hagenaars & A. L. McCutcheon (Eds.), *Applied latent class analysis* (pp. 3–55). Cambridge, UK: Cambridge University Press.

Heller, D. E. (1997). Student price response in higher education: An update to Leslie and Brinkman. *Journal of Higher Education*, 68(6), 624–659.

Huberty, C. J. (2005). Discriminant analysis. In B. S. Everett & D. C. Howell (Eds.), *Encyclopedia of statistics in behavioral science* (pp. 499–505). Chichester, England: Wiley.

Jung, T., & Wickrama, K. A. S. (2008). An introduction to latent class growth analysis and growth mixture modeling. *Social and Personality Psychology Compass*, 2(1), 302–317. doi:10.1111/j.1751-9004.2007.00054.x

Kim, D. (2007). The effect of loans on students' degree attainment: Differences by student and institutional characteristics. *Harvard Educational Review*, 77(1), 64–100.

Long, B. T. (2008). *What is known about the impact of financial aid? Implications for policy.* NCPR Working Paper. Retrieved from http://files.eric.ed.gov/fulltext/ED501555.pdf

Malcom, L. E., & Dowd, A. C. (2012). The impact of undergraduate debt on the graduate school enrollment of STEM baccalaureates. *Review of Higher Education*, 35(2), 265–305.

Masyn, K. (2013). Latent class analysis and finite mixture modeling. In T. Little (Ed.), *The Oxford handbook of quantitative methods in psychology* (Vol. 2, pp. 375–393). Oxford, England: Oxford University Press.

McCutcheon, A. L. (2002). Basic concepts and procedures in single- and multiple-group latent class analysis. In J. A. Hagenaars & A. L. McCutcheon (Eds.), *Applied latent class analysis* (pp. 56–89). Cambridge, England: Cambridge University Press.

McDonough, P. M., & Calderone, S. (2006). The meaning of money: Perceptual differences between college counselors and low-income families about college costs and financial aid. *American Behavioral Scientist*, 49(12), 1703–1718.

McLachlan, G. J., & Peel, D. (2000). *Finite mixture models.* New York, NY: Wiley.

Muthén, B., & Muthén, L. K. (2000). Integrating person-centered and variable-centered analyses: Growth mixture modeling with latent trajectory classes. *Alcoholism: Clinical and Experimental Research*, 24(6), 882–891.

Pastor, D. A. (2010). Cluster analysis. In G. R. Hancock & R. O. Mueller (Eds.), *The reviewer's guide to quantitative methods in the social sciences* (pp. 41–54). New York, NY: Routledge.

Pastor, D. A., Barron, K. E., Miller, B. J., & Davis, S. L. (2007). A latent profile analysis of college students' achievement goal orientation. *Contemporary Educational Psychology*, 32, 8–47.

Price, D. V. (2004). *Borrowing inequality: Race, class, and student loans.* Boulder, CO: Lynne Rienner.

Samuelsen, K. M., & Dayton, C. M. (2010). Latent class analysis. In G. R. Hancock & R. O. Mueller (Eds.), *The reviewer's guide to quantitative methods in the social sciences* (pp. 173–184). New York, NY: Routledge.

St. John, E. P. (2006). Contending with financial inequality and academic success: Rethinking the contributions of qualitative research to the policy discourse on college students. *American Behavioral Scientist*, 49(12), 1604–1619.

Stage, F. K. (2007). Asking critical questions using quantitative data. In F. K. Stage (Ed.), *New Directions for Institutional Research: No. 133. Using quantitative data to answer critical questions* (pp. 5–16). San Francisco, CA: Jossey-Bass.

Stage, F. K., & Wells, R. S. (2014). Critical quantitative inquiry in context. *New Directions for Institutional Research: No. 158. New scholarship in critical quantitative research—Part 1: Studying institutions and people in context* (pp. 1–7). San Francisco, CA: Jossey-Bass.

Weerts, D. J., Cabrera, A. F., & Mejias, P. P. (2013). Uncovering categories of civically engaged college students: A latent class analysis. *Review of Higher Education*, 37, 141–168.

LINDSEY MALCOM-PIQUEUX *is an assistant professor of higher education administration in the Graduate School of Education and Human Development at the George Washington University.*

5

This chapter discusses the importance of conducting critical social network analysis (CSNA) in higher education. To illustrate the benefits of CSNA, the authors use existing institutional data to examine peer effects in community colleges. The chapter ends with a discussion of the implications of using a CSNA approach to measure inequities in higher education.

Critical Social Network Analysis in Community Colleges: Peer Effects and Credit Attainment

Manuel S. González Canché, Cecilia Rios-Aguilar

The importance of social relationships has been highlighted in many of higher education's common models of access, persistence, and success, such as social and academic integration (Tinto, 1993), sense of belonging (Hurtado & Carter, 1997), experiences with diversity (Gurin, Dey, Hurtado, & Gurin, 2002), involvement (Astin, 1993), and engagement (Kuh, 2009). None of these concepts, however, has explicitly used social network theory and analysis (SNA)—the conceptual and statistical study of the structure of interaction as it occurs between persons and/or other social units (McFarland, Diehl, & Rawlings, 2011)—to critically examine how networks (and the resources embedded in them) influence students' educational and occupational trajectories.

Although the explosion of awareness about social networks has begun to spread to four-year institutions (see González Clarke & Antonio, 2012; Kollasch, 2013; O'Brien, 2011; Rios-Aguilar & Deil-Amen, 2012; Thomas, 2000), the use of social networks in community college settings remains undertheorized and understudied in a systematic and critical way. This chapter provides a concrete example of how a critical approach to SNA can be utilized to examine issues of equity in community colleges. Specifically, we provide researchers with tools to better understand course enrollment patterns and the influence of peers in those patterns at community colleges. From an institutional research perspective, these analyses are important because they capture the structure of networks among community college students using data routinely collected by institutions.

NEW DIRECTIONS FOR INSTITUTIONAL RESEARCH, no. 163 © 2015 Wiley Periodicals, Inc.
Published online in Wiley Online Library (wileyonlinelibrary.com) • DOI: 10.1002/ir.20087

We begin this chapter by presenting a brief history of SNA in higher education. We then introduce SNA more formally and explain basic terminology so our readers can follow our example more easily. We also discuss the importance of moving from SNA to *critical* SNA to help scholars and institutional researchers study equity issues in higher education. Next, we offer a concrete example of how to employ critical SNA with available institutional data to study peer effects in community colleges. We close our chapter by highlighting ways institutions and scholars should continue using critical SNA to examine inequities. Specifically, we show the diverse ways students from various subgroups (i.e., gender and race/ethnicity) are affected differently from their interactions with peers.

Brief History of SNA in Higher Education

Although the use of SNA in higher education began many years ago with the study of student (Newcomb, 1943) and faculty (Friedkin, 1978) networks, the available SNA scholarship in this field of study is scant and disjointed and rarely analyzes student networks (Biancani & McFarland, 2013). These features limit the potential impact of SNA in better understanding equity issues pertaining to postsecondary education. Moreover, *it was only very recently that* researchers started to offer a more critical and a mixed methods perspective of SNA. For example, Rios-Aguilar and Deil-Amen (2012) studied the networks of Latina/o students and found that their social network ties facilitated social capital relevant to getting into college, but such ties were less helpful in providing social capital useful for persisting in college and planning their professional trajectories. Another study (see González Clarke & Antonio, 2012) invites scholars to rethink scholarship that examines racial diversity and its impact on college students' outcomes. As with many studies, these authors' work focused on four-year institutions with no attention to issues affecting the millions of students who attend community colleges. Indeed, we have only very recently identified a handful of studies (e.g., Evans, McFarland, Rios-Aguilar, & Deil-Amen, 2014; González Canché, D'Amico, Rios-Aguilar, & Salas, 2014; O'Brien, 2011) that have begun to use SNA to examine issues of transfer, persistence, and success in two-year institutions. In summary, the current state of the scholarship in higher education relying on SNA is scant and overwhelmingly focused on the four-year sector.

We believe the use of SNA in higher education should become more systemic and holistic as its implementation in our field of study brings about many potential benefits. As suggested by McFarland et al. (2011), SNA can help higher education researchers by (1) applying network constructs in statistical models to better account for interdependencies, (2) reconceptualizing educational processes in terms of the fluid relationships between actors embedded in networks, and (3) revolutionizing the field by using technological breakthroughs in collecting and analyzing network data.

New Directions for Institutional Research • DOI: 10.1002/ir

However, if SNA is going to contribute to our field, it should also be conducted more carefully and from a critical perspective. Failing to do so will only exacerbate existing inequities by continuously blaming the oppressed for "lacking what it takes" to succeed in college. In this spirit, we add a fourth benefit: sustaining a critical, multidisciplinary, and multimethod examination of inequities in higher education. We call this approach *critical SNA (CSNA)*.

Why Is Critical SNA Important?

SNA, when used critically, allows us to move beyond an individualistic "perspective that has characterized much of educational and social scientific research in the past century" (Biancani & McFarland, 2013, p. 151). Social network analysts are first and foremost interested in how social structures encourage or constrain behaviors as a function of one's location in a given network (Wellman, 1983). SNA then becomes an ideal theoretical and empirical tool set to study how a person's place in a network affects her or his possibilities for connection formation and her or his associated opportunities for social mobility. Under this perspective, SNA is particularly relevant to critical quantitative scholars because it allows researchers to move from a deficit perspective on students (and organizations) to a richer understanding of how context and structures affect underrepresented students' opportunities in terms of access, persistence, and success in higher education.

As a critical endeavor, SNA must break with the vicious circle thinking that plagues most higher education research: Low-income, underprepared, nontraditional, and racial/ethnic minority community students do not persist and/or succeed because they do not have enough intellectual, intangible, and/or material resources and because they are not "engaged" in college. Many statistical models and conceptual frameworks ignore the complexities of people's lives and the extent to which decision making is a socially and historically embedded process rather than an individualized one (Fuller, Heath, & Johnston, 2011). Scholars need to shift their deficit mentality and stop defining people in terms of what they did not do (or what they did not possess). We must recognize that there are many pathways to success, and the higher education community should carefully examine these and validate the experiences of millions of marginalized students who are currently thinking of participating in higher education settings or currently enrolled in college. CSNA is both a theoretical and methodological toolbox that can help us to move in this direction. While the focus of our study is on CSNA, the following section describes the traditional SNA concepts upon our CSNA approach is build.

A More Technical Approach of SNA.   The term "social network analysis" refers to the methodology often employed to quantitatively study the connections actors or participants form with one another. To reiterate, SNA is the study of the patterns within a social structure. It is a methodological process often employed to study the connections of "nodes"—which denote actors that are usually individuals or organizations—via "ties." These ties or links represent the type of relationship that exists between two nodes (Knoke & Yang, 2008).

Due to its relational perspective, SNA integrates both societal micro and macro levels and offers a specific starting point for tracing the mechanisms of social integration as well as the conditions and implications of social change. The latter point implies two things. First, given that SNA is not only a methodological but also a theoretical tool, it must go beyond the "mathematization" (Carrington, 2014) of nodes and ties. Not only must SNA help us to describe, measure, and visualize networks, but it also must help us to understand agency and subjective attributions of meaning, norms, cultural practices, and symbolic worlds (Emirbrayer & Goodwin, 1994). Consequently, scholars need to be careful not to overly rely on measures (e.g., centrality, extensity, density) that describe the characteristics of the structure of the networks. They must also use the available conceptual network tools (e.g., social capital, strength of ties, homophily, network position, etc.) to comprehend why and how inequities keep reproducing in the higher education system.

SNA can (and should) also be studied from a mixed methods perspective. Only recently have researchers (e.g., Deil-Amen & Rios-Aguilar, 2014; Rios-Aguilar & Deil-Amen, 2012) incorporated information about the content and meaning of the ties they form (e.g., when actors explain the strategies of action they adopted, their own systems of relevance, perceptions, interpretations, and action orientations) and how these interact with social structure. This particular perspective on SNA can help researchers in higher education give voice to the experiences of underrepresented students (and their families and communities).

Basic SNA Terminology.   The definitions presented here are brief and are meant to facilitate the comprehension of the example elaborated in subsequent sections. These definitions are based on the seminal book of Wasserman and Faust (1994).

- *Actors/Nodes/Vertices* are the members of a network population. They can be anything from people (students, faculty, and staff) to organizations, events, and even words or concepts.
- *Ties/Edges/Links/Lines* are what connect the actors. These represent a vast range of relationships: (1) kinship: brother of, father of; (2) social roles: boss of, teacher of, friend of; (3) affective: likes, respects, hates; (4) cognitive: knows, views as similar, learns from, etc.; (5) actions: talks to, collaborates with, communicates with, etc.; (6) transfer of resources: financial aid transactions, enrollment patterns, advising sessions, etc.; (7) co-occurrence: is in the same class as, has the same race/ethnicity as, etc.

- *Network boundary definition* or *network population*. Before thinking of using or collecting any network data, the researcher must identify the population to be studied. In the case of a known set of actors (e.g., all students in a class or all students enrolled in a college), this issue is simple. However, the boundary of the set of actors may be difficult (if not impossible) to determine in cases where there are artificially occurring boundaries. Such would be the case when a researcher is interested in investigating students that live in a certain spatial area (defined as a living within a zip or census track) or students who live below the poverty line.
- *Types of networks*. Many different kinds of social networks can be studied, and Table 5.1 provides a description of each type. It is important to mention that all these sets of relationships can contain information on *actors/nodes/vertices* attributes. These attribute variables have the same nature as those measured in nonnetwork studies (typically contained in columns under variable names in data sets) and can be integrated into any type of network.

Importance of Two-Mode/Affiliation Networks. Since the publication of Breiger's (1974) seminal paper, network scholars have used the term "affiliation networks" to examine how membership or coparticipation in events provides (or denies) actors access to opportunities for social ties to develop, which in turn can provide opportunities for information and resources to flow between actors. Examples of affiliation data that have been found in the social sciences literature include membership in clubs (McPherson, 1982), participation in online groups (Allatta, 2003), and course-taking patterns of high school students (Frank et al., 2008). The cases of course-/credit-taking patterns and peer effects are particularly relevant for higher education because the data are readily available and can be examined from a (C)SNA perspective to measure inequities in the system.

As stated earlier, existing research focuses on the peer relations of college students in four-year institutions, neglecting other contexts. This chapter offers a relational/affiliation approach to studying peer effects in two-year institutions. This approach presents an opportunity to better examine the processes through which racial/ethnic diversity may (or may not) contribute to a variety of educational and social outcomes and, more important, to identify whether and how institutions facilitate this process.

Understanding the formal structures of peer network formation and affiliation from a gendered and racial/ethnic perspective[1] adds an important dimension to our current body of knowledge regarding the impact of peer social relationships on the college experience. A more intense focus on formal structures of peer network formation and affiliation within the college setting is clearly needed if we aspire to understand how underrepresented students can more successfully achieve their personal, academic, and professional goals.

Table 5.1. Description of Types of Networks

	One-Mode Complete Networks	Two-Mode Networks	Ego-Centered (or Personal) Networks
Actors: Students Classrooms Organizations Communities	One set of actors.	Two sets of actors, or One set of actors *and* One set of events (i.e., affiliation networks)	Focal actor called "ego" and a set of alters who have ties to ego.
		Note: The sets of actors can be of any type. Events can be activities, programs, classrooms, clubs, or organizations students are members of, etc.	Note: Usually the researcher uses a sampling technique to select egos and then asks egos to talk about their relations with alters.
Relations/ties: Kinship Social roles Affective Cognitive Actions Flows Transfer or resources Distance Co-occurrence Etc.	One or more relations can be measured for the single set of actors.	At least one relation is measured between actors in the two sets.	One or more relations can be measured for ego and his/her alters.

Attributes:
Gender
Race/ethnicity
Socioeconomic
  status
Immigration
  status
Etc.
	Can include one or many actor attributes	Can include actor attributes as well as event attributes (e.g., size of the club, location, etc.).	Can include one or many ego and alter attributes.

Note: Source of information used for building this table is Wasserman and Faust (1994).

Implementing a CSNA Perspective to Study Peer Effects in Community Colleges

As highlighted earlier in the chapter, network analysis aims at measuring the influence of actors within a given context. The purpose of the analysis presented herein is to assess whether the number of credits taken by one's classmates over the course of two academic years (Fall 2011–Summer 2013) has any effect on the number of credits she or he took during the same period. This is, under the network perspective, an empirical application of peer effects in which students may be influenced by their peers' course-/credit-taking patterns. Our case study was built from official administrative records gathered by institutions of higher education (IHEs). We place special emphasis on highlighting the structure of the data at every step of the cleaning process and the manner in which network principles allowed us to compute the models presented. The analyses were conducted in the R statistical environment, and all of the coding schemes and the computed algorithms are available on request should institutional researchers wish to conduct the same analyses (or similar ones) with their own data.

Context.   Calizona Community College (CCC) is located in a large city in the western region of the United States. The college enrolls approximately 25,000 students. Sixty percent of the student population is considered Latina/o, 29% is African American, 6% is White, and 5% is Asian American. Nearly 50% of the student population works more than 30 hours per week, and approximately the same percentage indicated that they are attending college for job preparation. CCC offers all the academic courses required for transfer to a four-year institution as well as nearly 90 different occupational programs. The student to counselor ratio is 702 to 1.

Data Cleaning and Preparation for CSNA.   All the data analyzed came from official institutional records that accounted for all students taking for-credit classes who enrolled in fall 2011. The final observations provided by CCC ended in summer 2013, representing two academic years or the corresponding time to attain a credential or accumulate enough credits to transfer to the four-year sector. We highlight that the models only accounted for credits completed by students; that is, before implementing the network-cleaning procedures, all classes enrolled that were dropped by students were excluded from the data. This was made possible given that there was a variable in the data indicating the date a given student officially *withdrew* a class.

The number of students represented in this 2011 to 2013 cohort was 7,324. During this period CCC offered 991 classes in which at least one of these 7,324 students enrolled. After dropping classes from which all students withdrew, the initial structure of the data resulted in what is shown in Figure 5.1. Note that on the left-hand side of the figure, we have three columns: one indicating the student identification number (ID), the second indicating the Class ID, and the third indicating the semester during which the student took a given class. Each Class ID is unique for a given semester; this means that had the institution offered two groups of the same class, a subindex would have indicated the specific section that a given student attended. This level of detail in the Class IDs ultimately allowed us to detect actual classmates, as detailed next.

Figure 5.1. Initial Transformation Followed in the Analytic Process

ID	ClassID	SemID
1	**Xrr**	**113**
1	Xrt	121
1	Vrt	113
2	**Xrr**	**113**
2	Erv	121
2	Fer	121
2	Web	121
...	...	...
N	*N*	*N*

Concatenation function applied to generate a composite class and semester ID

ID	ClassID+SemID
1	**xrr_113**
1	xrt_121
1	vrt_113
2	**xrr_113**
2	erv_121
2	fer_121
2	web_121
...	...
N	*N*

The first network procedure implemented was assigning each student to the classes enrolled in a given semester. To accomplish this, a concatenation function was created for Class ID and Semester ID, so that the composite ID of class and semester represents a unique ID that each student selected. The right-hand side of Figure 5.1 now shows the classes that each student took. This resulting list is also known in network analysis as an edge list or list of relationships. This list can represent a one-mode or two-mode network. As explained in Table 5.1, a one-mode network contains the same type of actors in the two columns that configure the edge list. In our case, the relationships reflected in the columns are between students and the classes they took in a given semester, thus representing a two-mode network. The information contained in the edge list can be transformed to a matrix form, which allowed us to conduct the manipulations required to continue with our analyses. Note that the transformation processes must not alter the original structural relationships of our dataset.

To continue with our example and to emphasize the preservation of the original relationships, we detail the process followed after the creation of the composite ID for class and semester. Specifically, we took the edge list shown on the right-hand side of Figure 5.1 and created a graph object. This graph object was then transformed to its matrix form as shown in Figure 5.2. To show the preservation of the original relationships, in Figure 5.1 note that participants with IDs 1 and 2 took one class in common (xrr) in Fall 2011 (coded 113 in the college records). The composite ID for this class is xrr_113 as highlighted with bold font in Figure 5.1. Consequently, Figure 5.2 must reflect this relationship as well while following a

Figure 5.2. Two-Mode Network Matrix Form of the Edge List Presented in Figure 5.1.

$$
\begin{bmatrix}
\text{ID} & \text{xrr\_113} & \text{xrt\_121} & \text{vrt\_113} & \text{erv\_121} & \text{fer\_121} & \text{web\_121} & \ldots & N \\
1 & 1 & 1 & 1 & 0 & 0 & 0 & \ldots & \ldots \\
2 & 1 & 0 & 0 & 1 & 1 & 1 & \ldots & \ldots \\
\ldots & \ldots & \ldots & \ldots & \ldots & \ldots & \ldots & \ldots & \ldots \\
N & \ldots & \ldots & \ldots & \ldots & \ldots & \ldots & \ldots & \ldots
\end{bmatrix}
$$

matrix form with the number of rows representing the total number of students and the number of columns accounting for the total number of class offerings during the period analyzed. In our actual data, the dimensions of the resulting matrix were 7,324 rows by 991 columns or [7324, 991].

For cases when a student enrolled in a class in a given semester, the intersection between row and column will have the numeral 1, indicating a presence of a relationship between the student and the class. When a student did not take a class, the corresponding intersecting cell will have the numeral 0. Following network principles, the sum of each row will tell us the total number of classes taken by each student, and the sum of each column will tell us the number of students who enrolled in a given class. In the example shown in Figure 5.2, we know that the student with ID 1 took three classes, whereas our student with ID 2 took four classes. We also know that these students took the class xrr_113 together. All of which was consistent with the information contained in the edge list in Figure 5.1.

The two-mode matrix presented in Figure 5.2 can be transformed further to a one-mode matrix. In this transformation, the analyst should decide which of the two relationships should be preserved in the resulting matrix: students or classes. For example, if the interest is in the classes that have the same participants, the resulting matrix would be a class-by-class matrix in which the diagonal will be the number of students in each class and the off-diagonal will be the number of students who took classes in common. Given that our interest is in the student-to-student relationships as a function of the classes they took in common, we decided to keep this relationship as shown in Figure 5.3. In this figure, note that the diagonal value represents the number of classes the students took during the period observed. Consistent with Figures 5.1 and 5.2, we see that student ID 1 took three classes and student ID 2 took four classes. We also can see that students 1 and 2 shared one class in common, but the name of this class is no longer known. Had students 1 and 2 shared more classes in common, the corresponding intersecting cell would have accounted for the number of classes shared.

The computation that allowed us to obtain Figure 5.3 follows $A * A^T$, where A is the two-mode matrix (Figure 5.2) and A^T is its transposed form.

Figure 5.3. One-Mode Network of the Matrix Represented in Figure 5.2

$$
\begin{bmatrix}
\text{ID} & 1 & 2 & \dots & N \\
1 & 3 & 1 & \dots & \dots \\
2 & 1 & 4 & \dots & \dots \\
\dots & \dots & \dots & \dots & \dots \\
N & \dots & \dots & \dots & \dots
\end{bmatrix}
$$

Based on matrix multiplication rules, the resulting matrix will have as the number of dimensions the number of rows of the first multiplier. In the data analyzed, the resulting matrix [7324, 7324] has 7,324 students in the rows and columns. In this matrix, the number of classes taken by each student is presented in the diagonal, and the number of classes each student took in common with other students is contained in the off-diagonal of the matrix.

Using the information contained in Figure 5.3, we proceeded to account for the effects of taking classes with peers that are more or less active in their credit-taking patterns. To accomplish this, we replaced the diagonal with zero, which nullifies the effect of each student taking classes with her- or himself. Recall that this diagonal contains the total number of classes each student took during the two academic years of data. In addition, we added an attribute to the matrix containing the number of credits each student took during the two years of data. This information was placed in a new column called "#creds i" in the matrix represented in Figure 5.3. After conducting these procedures, Figure 5.3 is now represented on the left-hand side of Figure 5.4.

With the information now contained on the left-hand side of Figure 5.4, we created an algorithm that counts the number of classmates a student had during her or his tenure in the institution and saved it in a new column called "#links." In addition, this algorithm takes the value of each cell of the column "#creds i" and substitutes it for each nonzero value in the

Figure 5.4. Diagonal Information Added as a Column and Changed to Zero to Avoid Self-Selection

ID	1	2	...	N	#creds i
1	0	1	...	...	9
2	1	0	...	...	12
...	...	...	...	...	...
N	...	...	...	...	...

⟹

ID	1	2	...	N	#creds i	#links	#creds j	#Avgpeer
1	0	9	...	...	9	n	x	x/n
2	12	0	...	...	12	n	y	y/n
...	...	...	...	...	...	...	...	.../...
N	...	...	...	...	...	...	...	.../...

entire relationship matrix. Note that, at this point, on the right-hand side of Figure 5.4 we show that the intersection between students with IDs 1 and 2 was replaced with 9 instead of 1. Note further that the intersection between student 2 and 1 is now 12. From the network perspective, the outdegree centrality (columns selecting rows) means the following: student ID 1, who attained nine credits, also took classes with student ID 2, who attained 12 credits. Student ID 2, who attained 12 credits, took classes with student ID 1, who completed nine credits. A simple sum of columns will render the total number of credits taken by the students j who took a class with student i, where j represents the classmates a student i had during the period observed. This information is recorded in the column called "#creds j." Finally, the ratio between columns "#creds j" and "#links" will render the average number of credits taken by the classmates that student i had during the period observed. The peer effects can then be measured (using ordinary least squares) by linear relationships between columns "#creds i" and "#creds j," which would tell us whether the average number of credits the classmates j of a student i have during this period had any effect in the number of credits such student i attained.

Adding Theory to the CSNA. Social network theory tells us that individuals tend to cluster together with similar individuals (Mark, 1998; McPherson, Smith-Lovin, & Cook, 2001), so it is unlikely that an aggregate estimation of this influence would render precise results. That is, just sitting in a class with a group of students does not necessarily translate into that group affecting our decisions to take more or fewer credits. We instead believe that our friendship or closeness to a certain subgroup of students would be more likely to do so. Given that students are more likely to get acquainted or even become friends with students from the same racial/ethnic group (Mark, 1998; McPherson et al., 2001), we expect that, when the models are disaggregated by race/ethnicity, our predictor and control variables will affect the variation of number of credits with different magnitudes.

To account for the effect of other important variables that may be masking/influencing our assumed relationships, we included the following control variables as provided by the institutional/official records: age, gender, major of study, veteran status, and financial aid recipient. The influence of academic major was included as a fixed effect in the regression models. Due to the number of majors (155 during this period), the summary statistics and the regression models excluded this indicator. This information is available on request.

Findings. The summary statistics of the outcome and control variables are discussed here, and the table is available on request. The average number of credits taken by a given student i was 38.16 (standard deviation [SD] $= 51.32$). The corresponding mean of the peer effects is 63.63 ($SD = 22.46$), meaning that, on average, students took credits with students j, who, on average, took 64 credits. The average age, as of the first semester observed, was 27 years ($SD = 10.51$ years). Note that 55% of the

NEW DIRECTIONS FOR INSTITUTIONAL RESEARCH • DOI: 10.1002/ir

Table 5.2. Peer Effects on Number of Credits Taken

	Aggregate	White	Asian	Hispanic	Af/Am
(Intercept)	−5.74	8.89	13.46	−3.06	−2.62
	(3.04)	(4.69)	(7.11)	(3.84)	(5.29)
Peer effects (creds j)	0.32***	0.31***	0.33***	0.35***	0.10*
	(0.03)	(0.05)	(0.06)	(0.04)	(0.05)
Age (years)	0.27***	−0.10	−0.14	0.25*	0.46***
	(0.06)	(0.12)	(0.19)	(0.11)	(0.10)
Veteran	1.34	5.93	7.96	−0.45	−2.95
	(3.19)	(5.71)	(12.54)	(5.54)	(5.71)
BOGG[a]	9.31**	38.16***	10.19	5.83	11.48*
	(3.26)	(10.38)	(15.74)	(4.63)	(5.58)
Pell	25.58***	0.04	14.80	28.50***	27.93***
	(3.24)	(10.20)	(15.62)	(4.57)	(5.75)
Aid other	1.57	−28.28**	−13.05	5.24	5.84
	(3.46)	(10.87)	(16.12)	(5.00)	(6.34)
Female	4.93***	−0.31	−0.39	4.43*	7.97**
	(1.27)	(3.13)	(3.89)	(1.84)	(2.57)
Hispanic[b]	4.06*				
	(1.93)				
Asian[b]	2.11				
	(2.55)				
Af/Am[b]	−2.38				
	(2.08)				
R^2	0.17	0.34	0.28	0.18	0.15
Adj. R^2	0.15	0.27	0.17	0.15	0.10
Number of observations	7,324	770	626	3,784	2,144

***$p < 0.001$, **$p < 0.01$, *$p < 0.05$.
[a]Board of Governors Grant (BOGG).
[b]White is the comparison group.
All the models include the fixed effects of major of study.

participants received the Board of Governors Grant (BOGG), 29% received a Pell grant, and 29% received any other form of financial aid. We also saw that half of the student body was Hispanic (51%) and that the second most represented group was African American students (29%). Female students accounted for 41% of the student cohort analyzed. Finally, veteran students only accounted for 3% of the cohort participants.

Table 5.2 reports the regression model results. The first model aggregates all races and ethnicities; here the assumption is that the presence of students taking x number of credits may affect a student's i number of credits attained. As we expected, the coefficient associated with peer effects shows a significant relationship between these two variables. This model, however, shows further that female, Hispanic, and Pell and BOGG grant recipients tend to have higher credits on average. The remaining models are disaggregated by race/ethnicity. The associations between peer effects and the number of credits taken across models were positive and statistically significant. African American students were the least influenced group as the magnitude of peer effects was a third of the magnitude found across the models. In the case of African American students, we can conclude that, after controlling for financial aid, age, veteran status, and major of study, for every 10 credit increase on average that their peers had, African American students increased only one extra credit. In the case of the White, Asian, and Hispanic participants, the effect of the peer effects was the following: *ceteris paribus*, for every three credits their peers of the same race took on average, these students took one extra credit.

Two other variables affected African American and Hispanic students differently than their White and Asian counterparts. The first is that Pell grant, an indicator highly related to low–socioeconomic status backgrounds, was statistically significant only for Hispanic and African American students (or minority/underrepresented students in higher education). For these students, receiving Pell grant aid was associated with an increase in almost 30 credits during this two-year period. The second indicator that presented significant variation across racial/ethnic groups was gender, indicating that female Hispanic and African American students tended to have more credits than their male counterparts. Based on these two differences,[2] it is expected that the intersection between gender and ethnicity is playing an important role in affecting this relationship between peer effects and credits attained. To test for the magnitudes of these effects, we conducted four final models presented in Table 5.3.

Table 5.3 highlights the importance of further disaggregating the models by the intersection of race/ethnicity and gender. Note that no peer effects were found for female Hispanic and female African American students. That is, for them, taking classes with other female Hispanic and female African American students was not related to the variation in the number of credits attained, *ceteris paribus*. In the case of Hispanic males, the coefficient was the highest found, meaning that for every two credits their male Hispanic peers took, a male Hispanic student took one extra credit on average, a relationship that was also highly significant. The relationship found among male African American students was much more modest in magnitude but still statistically significant. It is important to note that, in all the models, the effect of Pell grant was positive and statistically significant with an average effect of more than 30 credits for male participants and above 20 credits for female students.

Discussion

These findings reveal important trends. First, students at CCC attend a college in which 80% of the student body belongs to minority, underrepresented groups in higher education (Hispanic and African American). We also found that these minority students were the only groups that were positively affected by the receipt of a Pell grant, which highlights their

Table 5.3. Peer Effects on Number of Credits Taken by Minority and Gender Intersection

	Female/Hispanic	Male/Hispanic	Female/AfAm	Male/AfAm
(Intercept)	8.15	−6.05	7.48	−5.38
	(7.35)	(4.07)	(8.83)	(6.00)
Peer Effects (creds j)	0.09	0.49***	0.05	0.16**
	(0.06)	(0.04)	(0.07)	(0.06)
Age (years)	0.68**	0.13	0.52**	0.50***
	(0.23)	(0.11)	(0.18)	(0.12)
Veteran	7.92	−0.75	3.31	−4.04
	(18.82)	(5.45)	(21.29)	(5.62)
BOGG[a]	8.63	1.65	19.30*	5.26
	(7.88)	(5.78)	(8.63)	(7.51)
Pell	26.51***	30.85***	21.78*	30.54***
	(7.85)	(5.67)	(9.14)	(7.62)
Aid other	2.28	9.50	−1.63	10.10
	(8.64)	(6.18)	(10.05)	(8.36)
R^2	0.15	0.24	0.15	0.19
Adj. R^2	0.10	0.19	0.07	0.11
Number of observations	1,430	2,342	1,024	1,101

***$p < 0.001$, **$p < 0.01$, *$p < 0.05$.
[a]Board of Governors Grant (BOGG).
All the models include the fixed effects of major of study.

propensity to come from low-income backgrounds. Previous research has found that African American and Latina/o students who attend intensely segregated community colleges and come from low-income backgrounds are less likely to transfer to four-year colleges (Martínez-Wenzl & Marquez, 2012). Instead of focusing on a deficit perspective, using CSNA we found that male African American and male Latino students are benefiting from interacting with similar peers (i.e., peers from the same racial/ethnic group) in terms of the credits they complete and, most likely, in terms of the networks they form. It seems that one way to entice male minority students to complete more credits would be to place them with students who tend to have higher credits accumulated, a strategy that, based on our analyses, would not work with female minority students. Hispanic and female African American students are not affected by their peers in the variation of credits attained. In closing, our findings have important financial and academic implications for minority students, with divergent impact conditional on gender, an issue that requires further exploration.

Implications for Institutional Researchers

From an institutional research perspective, these analyses are important because they capture the structure of networks among community college students with data that are routinely collected by institutions using software that is freely available. We hope that institutional researchers will incorporate these analytic techniques in their own institutional settings to better inform decisions regarding course offerings and services offered to students to help them persist and graduate.

CSNA can (and should) also be studied from a mixed methods perspective. A more in-depth qualitative exploration of the findings presented in this study would be ideal to give voice to the experiences of underrepresented students (and their families and communities) and might also reveal a clearer story about the intersection of race and gender. Nonetheless, our quantitative findings, based on CSNA, do reveal important patterns that move beyond a deficit-oriented perspective that is typical of much of the research that is cross-sectional and has not utilized CSNA techniques to capture influence. Although we learned that peer effects only influence one gender in underrepresented groups, we are missing the reason for why that is happening, which would need to be part of another analysis. It is, however, important to highlight that our approach is completely replicable and reproducible, and other institutional researchers should take advantage of data they already have that can be analyzed via the network perspective.

Notes

1. This rationale can be expanded to include other group of students that traditionally have been classified as vulnerable or at risk, such as gay and lesbian students, and even students with disabilities.

2. This was not the case for Asian and White participants. Consequently, these models did not need to be disaggregated.

References

Allatta, J. (2003). Structural analysis of communities of practice: An investigation of job title, location, and management intention. In M. Huysman, E. Wegner, & V. Wulf (Eds.), *Communities and technologies* (pp. 23–42). Amsterdam, the Netherlands: Kluwer Academic.

Astin, A. (1993). *What matters in college? Four critical years revisited.* San Francisco, CA: Jossey-Bass.

Biancani, S., & McFarland, D. (2013). Social networks research in higher education. *Higher Education Handbook of Theory and Research, 28,* 151–216.

Breiger, R. L. (1974). The duality of persons and groups. *Social Forces, 53*(2), 181–190.

Carrington, P. (2014). Social network research. In S. Dominguez & B. Hollstein (Eds.), *Mixed methods social networks research: Design and applications* (pp. 35–64). New York, NY: Cambridge University Press.

Deil-Amen, R., & Rios-Aguilar, C. (2014). From FAFSA to Facebook: The role of technology in navigating the financial aid process. In A. Kelly & S. Goldrick-Rab (Eds.), *Reinventing financial aid: Charting a new course to college affordability* (pp. 75–100). Harvard Education Press.

Emirbayer, M., & Goodwin, J. (1994). Network analysis, culture, and the problem of agency. *American Journal of Sociology, 99*(6), 1411–1445.

Evans, E., McFarland, D., Rios-Aguilar, C., & Deil-Amen, R. (2014). *Community (in) colleges: The relationship between on-line network involvement and academic persistence at a community college.* Unpublished manuscript.

Frank, K. A., Muller, C., Schiller, K. S., Riegle-Crumb, C., Mueller, A. S., Crosnoe, R., & Pearson, J. (2008). The social dynamics of course taking in high school. *American Journal of Sociology, 113*(6), 1645–1696.

Friedkin, N. E. (1978). University social structure and social networks among scientists. *American Journal of Sociology, 83*(6), 1444–1465.

Fuller, A., Heath, S., & Johnston, B. (Eds.). (2011). *Rethinking widening participation in higher education: The role of social networks.* New York, NY: Routledge.

González Canché, M., D'Amico, M., Rios-Aguilar, C., & Salas, S. (2014). It's who you know: Leveraging social networks for college and careers. *Community College Enterprise, 20*(1), 18–35.

González Clarke, C., & Antonio, A. (2012). Re-thinking research on the impact of racial diversity in higher education. *Review of Higher Education, 36*(1), 25–50.

Gurin, P., Dey, E., Hurtado, S., & Gurin, G. (2002). Diversity and higher education: Theory and impact on educational outcomes. *Harvard Educational Review, 72*(3), 330–366.

Hurtado, S., & Carter, D. (1997). Effects of college transition and perceptions of the campus racial climate on Latino college students' sense of belonging. *Sociology of Education, 70,* 324–345.

Knoke, D., & Yang, S. (2008). *Social network analysis* (2nd ed.). Thousand Oaks, CA: Sage.

Kollasch, A. (2013). *Ties that bind international research teams: A network multilevel model of interdisciplinary collaboration* (Unpublished doctoral dissertation). University of Arizona, Tucson.

Kuh, G. (2009). What student affairs professionals need to know about student engagement. *Journal of College Student Development, 50*(6), 683–706.

Mark, N. (1998). Birds of a feather sing together. *Social Forces, 77*(2), 453–485.

Martínez-Wenzl, M., & Marquez, R. (2012). *Unrealized promises: Unequal access, affordability, and excellence at community colleges in Southern California.* UCLA Civil Rights Project. Retrieved from http://civilrightsproject.ucla.edu/research/metro-and-regional-inequalities/lasanti-project-los-angeles-san-diego-tijuana

McFarland, D., Diehl, D., & Rawlings, C. (2011). Methodological transactionalism and the sociology of education. In M. Hallinan (Ed.), *Frontiers of the sociology of education* (pp. 87–109). New York, NY: Springer.

McPherson, J. (1982). Hypernetwork sampling: Duality and differentiation among voluntary organizations. *Social Networks, 3,* 225–249.

McPherson, J., Smith-Lovin, L., & Cook, J. M. (2001). Birds of a feather: Homophily in social networks. *Annual Review of Sociology, 27,* 415–444.

Newcomb, T. M. (1943). *Personality and social change: Attitude formation in a student community.* New York, NY: Dryden Press.

O'Brien, C. (2011). *Navigating the transition: The informational networks and help-seeking behavior of community college transfer students* (Unpublished doctoral dissertation). University of Arizona, Tucson.

Rios-Aguilar, C., & Deil-Amen, R. (2012). Beyond getting in and fitting in: An examination of social networks and professionally relevant social capital among Latina/o university students. *Journal of Hispanic Higher Education, 20*(10), 1–18.

Thomas, S. L. (2000). Ties that bind: A social network approach to understanding student integration and persistence. *Journal of Higher Education, 71*(5), 591–615.

Tinto, V. (1993). *Leaving college: Rethinking the causes and cures of student attrition.* Chicago, IL: University of Chicago Press.

Wasserman, S., & Faust, K. (1994). *Social network analysis: Methods and applications.* New York, NY: Cambridge University Press.

Wellman, B. (1983). Network analysis: Some basic principles. In R. Collins (Ed.), *Sociological theory* (pp. 155–200). San Francisco, CA: Jossey-Bass.

MANUEL S. GONZÁLEZ CANCHÉ *is an assistant professor of higher education at the Institute of Higher Education at the University of Georgia.*

CECILIA RIOS-AGUILAR *is an associate professor of education at the School of Educational Studies at Claremont Graduate University.*

NEW DIRECTIONS FOR INSTITUTIONAL RESEARCH • DOI: 10.1002/ir

If quantitative criticalism is thought to be a bridge between positivist epistemologies prevalent in quantitative work and social constructionism often found in critical qualitative work, then this bridge is fraught with challenges and tensions. This chapter examines the methodological issues, questions, and tensions that emerged from a research team project. What constitutes "good" research? To what extent do we take our critical perspective in our analysis? Is quantitative criticalism a coming together of different research paradigms? What training is essential for quantitative criticalist work? These critical methodological questions require some frank discussion as we move forward in developing research designs that incorporate quantitative criticalism and in training new researchers.

What Is "Good" Research? Revealing the Paradigmatic Tensions in Quantitative Criticalist Work

Ebelia Hernández

> You got to know the rules to break them. That's what I'm here for—to demolish the rules but keep tradition.
>
> —Alexander McQueen

Fall 2011 was a significant time for me. Two events influenced my thinking about a research project that I was developing alongside Michael Mobley that used Student Experience in the Research University (SERU) survey data on college student engagement (Hernández, Mobley, Coryell, Yu, & Martinez, 2013). The first was my attendance at the Alexander McQueen exhibit at the Metropolitan Museum of Art. In addition to seeing great works of art, I learned about the fashion designer's training, which included an apprenticeship at London's renowned Savile Row, where he learned the precision and skill in tailoring suits that later helped him deconstruct without losing structure or integrity of the garment. This approach of mastering the rules well enough to know how to break them stayed with me.

New Directions for Institutional Research, no. 163 © 2015 Wiley Periodicals, Inc.
Published online in Wiley Online Library (wileyonlinelibrary.com) • DOI: 10.1002/ir.20088

93

The second significant event was a preconference workshop at the annual conference of the Association for the Study of Higher Education, where I was introduced to the quantitative criticalist approach. I struggled with how to connect my use of critical race theory (CRT) into the SERU study. I wanted to move away from traditionally prescribed analytic strategies of comparing levels of engagement between different racial groups and without following the normative definition of engagement that has been grounded in a largely White, middle-class student population. Olivas (2011) warned that such approaches may perpetuate inequities and misrepresentation of minoritized populations. My agenda to challenge the normative, analytic processes used for institutional survey data was validated by quantitative criticalism that endorses the task to "question the models, measures, and analytic processes and outcomes on a large scale to reveal inequities" (Stage, 2007, p. 10).

I went back to the research team excited to implement quantitative criticalism into the SERU study. It seemed like it would be an easy process of integrating our complementary strengths—Michael's expertise in "quantitative research"[1] with my experience of conducting research on college student engagement with a CRT perspective. However, we did not realize what we were getting ourselves into—there was no methodology text to explain the practical and theoretical methodological tensions that can emerge or to foretell the practical considerations of manuscript writing and publication when a critical theoretical perspective is applied to analytic techniques grounded in a positivistic epistemology tradition.

This chapter reviews the methodological issues that arose from our research project and takes on the task set forth by Rios-Aguilar (2014) for quantitative criticalists to engage in methodological self-reflection to examine our own research practices, the factors that influence our practice, and how we can improve it. My aim is to move the conversation about methodology forward—from focusing on the legitimacy and usefulness of critical quantitative research as addressed in the first volume of *New Directions in Institutional Research* that introduced quantitative criticalism published in 2007, and even from the focus of Stage and Wells (2014) on expanding the notion of critical quantitative inquiry, toward a focus on grappling with paradigmatic concerns that require attention in order to ensure rigor and appropriate training for the application of quantitative criticalism.

Quantitative Criticalism's Paradigmatic Shift in Quantitative Studies

To demonstrate the value of quantitative criticalism, the focus of the first volume on quantitative criticalism in *New Directions in Institutional Research* (Stage, 2007) was to demonstrate how a critical perspective could raise new research questions that could reveal flaws in our normative research practices. For the moment, the conversation about methods was placed in the background so that attention could be focused on the potential usefulness of quantitative criticalism. This process of initially focusing on the potential contributions of a new methodology rather than the philosophical and methodological implications mirrors the evolution of mixed-methods research (Creswell & Plano Clark, 2011). Similar to quantitative criticalism, mixed methods has faced challenges in gaining recognition as a legitimate methodology because it does not clearly fall into the traditions of "quantitative research" or "qualitative research" (Morgan, 2007). This difficulty of not being easily categorized within into either research tradition leads to questions that, left unanswered, may challenge the soundness of a quantitative criticalist approach.

Upon reflecting on my own work with the SERU study and the growing body of research that has employed quantitative criticalism, I identified three methodological challenges that emerged. These challenges require further thought and unfortunately are not easily resolved. The focus here is not to find definitive solutions but to create dialogue among researchers that can lead to challenging normative practices and assumptions about what is "good" research, which may provide a more solid foundation on which quantitative criticalism can rest. These three challenges are:

1. Quantitative criticalism challenges normative assumptions and research practices in "quantitative research."
2. Quantitative criticalism requires a high level of expertise in both statistical analyses *and* critical theory.
3. Quantitative criticalism requires the use of a set of critical theoretical tenets to ensure legitimacy and rigor.

Next, I examine each of these methodological challenges by connecting them to the larger dialogue on research methodology and considering how these challenges emerged in our SERU research project.

Quantitative Criticalism Challenges Normative Assumptions About "Quantitative Research"

Quantitative criticalism has been met with resistance from the general research community, faculty, and journal editors because it does not fall neatly into the "quantitative research" paradigm (Stage & Wells, 2014). Quantitative criticalism disrupts the tradition of using what Guba and Lincoln (2005) refer to as *conventional* epistemologies, defined as research practices that are grounded in positivism and found predominantly in studies that use quantitative data. Aside from the general discomfort of moving away from conventional methodologies, there are substantive methodological reasons for the resistance against combining critical epistemologies with quantitative data and analytic processes.

The first issue is the assumed mismatch between criticalist epistemology and positivistic analytic strategies. Statistical analytic practices, which are grounded in a positivistic epistemology, aim to examine generalizations about a sample; outliers are unimportant; and the focus is on a majority rather than the minority. These aims seem to run counter to quantitative criticalism, which aims to "consciously choos[e] questions that seek to challenge" (Stage, 2007, p. 8) and to develop analytic practices that can better represent the misrepresented, such as minoritized students of color (p. 10). Do quantitative criticalists move from one epistemology to another by using a criticalist perspective to create research questions, taking a positivist epistemological stance to "run the data" and then returning to criticalism to interpret the data?

Although moving from one similar epistemology to another in the same study may be considered a possibility, specifically in mixed-methods research where each data collection method may be grounded in different epistemological frameworks (Creswell & Plano Clark, 2011), this does not seem to be the case with quantitative criticalism. Additionally, using two dissimilar, opposing epistemologies in one study compromises the integrity of research (Guba & Lincoln, 2005). Indeed, there is evidence of the central role that critical epistemology plays in quantitative criticalism. The social justice agenda and axiology (values of critical researchers) are embedded, not external, to our quantitative criticalist stance, which informs what we choose to study, the kinds of questions we ask, and how we go about research, including data collection and analysis (see Guba & Lincoln, 2005, p. 265). A strong example of explicitly describing how a critical epistemology informed research questions and design is Oseguera and Hwang's (2014) study of college education trajectories of low-income students.

As featured in Stage and Wells (2014), quantitative criticalists have worked within the positivistic paradigm to use statistical analysis in a way that repositions who is identified as the majority in their data by moving away from norming on White, middle-class students to students of color to reconsider the experiences of minoritized populations (e.g., Latinas/os, immigrants, low-income students). Indeed, this work supports Lincoln and Guba's (1985) conclusion that "there are many opportunities for the naturalistic investigator to utilize quantitative data—probably more than appreciated" (p. 199).

When one chooses to follow the norms of "quantitative research," there are comfort and validation in doing "good" research by following a prescribed process of conducting the research and writing the results for publication. When we decided to employ a quantitative criticalist approach, we did not have a formula to follow. We were excited to try unconventional approaches but also recognized that we were still researchers who sought endorsement from the higher education methodological community (Rios-Aguilar, 2014). Much of this "quantitative research" works within a positivistic paradigm and is based on "shared beliefs . . . [and] a consensus about which questions are most meaningful and which procedures are most appropriate for answering those questions" (Morgan, 2007, p. 53). The big question for us was how innovative we could be while still meeting the methodological community's expectations of "good research." Which conventions must be followed, and which were open for modification?

The published work of Teranishi (2007) and of Solórzano, Villalpando, and Oseguera (2005) gave us legitimacy to use CRT in quantitative studies;[2] however, there were no exemplars outside the first *New Directions in Institutional Research* (Stage, 2007) volume that explicitly referenced quantitative criticalism. I conducted several literature searches and even emailed the editor of a top-tier journal to ask for exemplars of quantitative criticalism, but I could not find any. The search for examples had a practical purpose: How could I write up a study that employed a critical quantitative stance and used a critical race theoretical perspective? What language and research components are appropriate? Should we use Lincoln and Guba's (1985) naturalistic terminologies and components based on naturalistic epistemologies, or the positivistic language that is the norm of statistical studies?

My prior scholarship using CRT included sections on epistemology, theoretical perspective, and positionality to explain the role that CRT played in my research and the racialized power dynamics within the research project itself. It was difficult to determine if these sections, routinely included in qualitative studies, should be included and, if so, to what extent. How do I word them? Ultimately, we included a section about CRT as a theoretical perspective and an explanation of quantitative criticalism as our research stance because there was precedence in published work that we could cite. We did not include epistemology or positionality as there seemed to be no precedent for it in peer-reviewed, published quantitative research papers. However, the growing scholarship featured in Part 1 of *New Scholarship in Critical Quantitative Research* (Stage & Wells, 2014) challenges these norms of how to write quantitative studies. Authors in that publication clearly articulated quantitative criticalism as a theoretical framework. The chapter by Alcantar (2014) included another element typically found in publications from qualitative studies. Alcantar examined her own reflexivity—which Schwandt (2007) defines as "the process of critical self-reflection on one's biases, theoretical predispositions, and so forth" to place the "full presence of the writer in the text" (p. 260)—to explain how her experiences as a low-income first-generation student informed her revision of civic engagement measures for Latina/o students.

Quantitative Criticalism Requires a High Level of Expertise in Statistical Analyses and Critical Theory

When researchers use a hybrid methodology, how well trained should they be to do "good" research? Various scholars have weighed in. Going back to mixed-methods research, there is an expectation that those who wish to do mixed methods should be, at minimum, acquainted with both quantitative and qualitative data collection and analysis techniques (Creswell & Plano Clark, 2011). Stage (2007), however, concluded that a high level of quantitative analytic skill is required to do "good" quantitative criticalist work because "researchers inexperienced with quantitative approaches might not recognize or understand the detailed measurement of some variables, the effects of ignoring other variables, and the implications of positional placements of variables in causal models," which then could result in missing the hidden assumptions embedded in data and perpetuation of inequities (p. 9).

Critics have also demanded a stronger theoretical grounding and understanding of critical theory to achieve the equity goals that are part of the practice of using critical theory (Pasque, Carducci, Gildersleeve, & Kuntz, 2011). Critical theorists challenge how well critical theory is used in our work—is it relegated to being merely a methodological component, or is it embedded in the study where it informs all aspects of the research process? I recall a symposium at the American Educational Research Association (AERA) where CRT scholars challenged researchers to move away from superficially using CRT—mentioning it in the literature review, focusing the study on a minoritized student population—to a more substantive application where it informs data collection and analytic strategies to engage the community that is being studied by including its participation into the research process and/or sharing the findings to help inform change. Indeed, critics of quantitative criticalism seem to voice this concern as well: Quantitative criticalists may not fully comprehend or commit to the full use of critical theory because a lack of evidence details how this work seeks to transform, or at least engage with, the communities they represent. Rios-Aguilar (2014) reminded us that at the heart of critical theorists is an active social justice agenda. How is our work transformative? How are we giving back to the community we are representing in our work? Certainly qualitative studies that use critical theories may lend themselves more easily to establishing and maintaining connections with these communities via the data collection and analysis process (e.g., interviews, focus groups, member checking). Quantitative studies do not have these advantages, yet we must include transformative components to ensure rigor and substantive use of critical theory in our research.

Quantitative criticalists also have two communities to whom they must answer. It is not enough to be strong in quantitative studies *or* critical theory. I argue that we need to be masters of the rules that both communities use to determine what "good" research is. In reflecting on my experience with the SERU study, I recognize that familiarity with quantitative research was not enough; I relied too heavily on Michael's statistical expertise. The plan for our strengths to complement each other was, on the surface, a great idea. But, in the end, I realized that scholars should have more than familiarity with quantitative research and critical theory; rather, mastery is required in order to demolish the rules but keep tradition.

Qualitative Criticalism Requires the Use of a Set of Critical Theoretical Standards/Tenets to Ensure Legitimacy and Rigor

The growing body of quantitative criticalist research is creating footholds in both the quantitative and critical theory methodological research communities. As more research is being published that explicitly uses the term "quantitative criticalism," the approach is gaining legitimacy as a viable approach to research. The ability for new scholars to cite this work to substantiate their own use of quantitative criticalism is a significant advantage that is exciting and promising. To that end, it is essential for scholars who use critical approaches in their work to continue publishing works that explicitly indicate the use of critical theoretical perspectives.

Moving forward, there is still significant work to be done to ensure the rigor of this type of equity work in higher education. I propose an additional task to those that Stage and Wells (2014) identified as essential for quantitative criticalism, which are to (1) use quantitative data to reveal educational inequities and institutional perpetuation of racism; (2) challenge the models, measures, and analytic practices to develop new processes that may better represent minoritized populations; and (3) conduct culturally relevant research by examining institutions and students in context (p. 3). Considering that quantitative scholars need to be masters of both quantitative methods and critical theory, a fourth task—the use of critical theory tenets to develop and inform the research project—is warranted so that scholars clearly define what "critical" means to them, what they are critical about, and how their definition has informed their work.

Reflecting back to how I have used Solórzano's (1998) CRT tenets as a foundation to inform my methodological choices and interpretation of findings, inclusion of these tenets into my writing also connects my work to the CRT methodological community. These five tenets, which are inclusive of LatCrit and are grounded in educational research, are (1) the centrality of race and racism and intersection with other forms of subordination; (2) the challenge to dominant ideology; (3) the commitment to social justice; (4) the centrality of experiential knowledge; and (5) the interdisciplinary perspective (Solórzano, 1998). My application of these tenets to the development and analytic process of the SERU study strengthened my work as a quantitative criticalist because it provided the ingredients needed to develop a rigorous, critical empirical study and ensured my credibility as an equity-minded scholar. For example, applying the CRT tenet of challenging dominant ideologies provided me the inspiration and theoretical legitimacy to challenge the normative definition of student engagement, which has been defined largely by research centered on White, middle-class students.

My use of CRT tenets also defines what "critical" means to me. CRT has informed the questions that I ask, the methods I choose, and the agenda that I seek to pursue as an equity-minded scholar focused on uncovering racism and its effects in the educational experiences of minoritized students. Other scholars have clearly connected their work to specific critical theories to explain what "critical" means to them and how their chosen theoretical frameworks have informed their work. Kinzie's (2007) critical feminist perspective defined the critical lens she used to examine women's paths in science. Her feminist theoretical perspective informed the kinds of questions she asked and gave her *methodological commitments* that informed her research design, such as investigating power relationships and exposing oppression. Stage (2007) defined her conceptualization of critical from Kincheloe and McLaren's (1994) work on critical social science.

Conclusion

This chapter considers three methodological challenges that quantitative criticalism presents. These challenges have emerged as a result of quantitative criticalism's challenging the status quo of the "quantitative research" community in regard to what is considered "good" research. These challenges also indicate that doing rigorous critical research that uses quantitative data is difficult because it requires mastery in both quantitative research and critical theory. Critiques by both quantitative research scholars and criticalists can be addressed with more transparency in our writing. We need to explicitly state our methodological choices and the theoretical underpinnings that inform our critical approaches. Scholars who wish to take on quantitative criticalism should be well trained not only to understand the paradigmatic tensions that arise from this kind of approach, but also to be able to work within it and explain how they have done so. In the end, the effort is worthwhile and necessary in order to transform the way we think about and use quantitative studies.

Notes

1. Following Morgan's (2007) example, the terms "quantitative research" and "qualitative research" are designated with quotation marks to refer them as paradigmatic traditions, which are distinct from quantitative and qualitative data methods.
2. The term "quantitative studies" refers here to studies that use quantitative data.

References

Alcantar, C. M. (2014). Civic engagement measure for Latina/o college students. In F. K. Stage & R. S. Wells (Eds.), *New Directions for Institutional Research: No. 158. New scholarship in critical quantitative research—Part 1: Studying institutions and people in context* (pp. 23–35). San Francisco, CA: Jossey-Bass.

Creswell, J. W., & Plano Clark, V. L. (2011). *Designing and conducting mixed methods research* (2nd ed.). Thousand Oaks, CA: Sage.

Guba, E. G., & Lincoln, Y. S. (2005). Paradigmatic controversies, contradictions, and emerging confluences. In N. K. Denzin & Y. S. Lincoln (Eds.), *The landscape of qualitative research: Theories and issues* (2nd ed., pp. 253–291). Thousand Oaks, CA: Sage.

Hernández, E., Mobley, M., Coryell, G., Yu, E.-H., & Martinez, G. (2013). Examining the cultural validity of a college student engagement survey for Latinos. *Journal of Hispanic Higher Education, 12*(2), 153–173.

Kincheloe, J. L., & McLaren, P. L. (1994). Rethinking critical theory and qualitative research. In N. Denzin & Y. Lincoln (Eds.), *Handbook of qualitative research* (pp. 138–157). London, UK: Sage.

Kinzie, J. (2007). Women's paths in science: A critical feminist analysis. In F. K. Stage (Ed.), *New Directions for Institutional Research: No. 133. Using quantitative data to answer critical questions* (pp. 81–93). San Francisco, CA: Jossey-Bass.

Lincoln, Y. S., & Guba, E. G. (1985). *Naturalistic inquiry*. Beverly Hills, CA: Sage.

Morgan, D. L. (2007). Paradigms lost and pragmatism regained: Methodological implications of combining qualitative and quantitative methods. *Journal of Mixed Methods Research, 1*(2), 48–76.

Olivas, M. A. (2011). If you build it, they will assess it (or, an open letter to George Kuh, with love and respect). *Review of Higher Education, 35*(1), 1–15.

Oseguera, L., & Hwang, J. (2014). Using large data sets to study college education trajectories. In F. K. Stage & R. S. Wells (Eds.), *New Directions for Institutional Research: No. 158. New scholarship in critical quantitative research—Part 1: Studying institutions and people in context* (pp. 37–50). San Francisco, CA: Jossey-Bass.

Pasque, P. A., Carducci, R., Gildersleeve, R. E., & Kuntz, A. M. (2011). Disrupting the ethical imperatives of "junior" critical qualitative scholars in the era of conservative modernization. *Qualitative Inquiry, 17*(7), 571–588.

Rios-Aguilar, C. (2014). The changing context of critical quantitative inquiry. In F. K. Stage & R. S. Wells (Eds.), *New Directions for Institutional Research: No. 158. New scholarship in critical quantitative research—Part 1: Studying institutions and people in context* (pp. 95–107). San Francisco, CA: Jossey-Bass.

Schwandt, T. A. (2007). *The Sage dictionary of qualitative inquiry* (3rd ed.). Thousand Oaks, CA: Sage.

Solórzano, D. G. (1998). Critical race theory, race and gender microaggressions, and the experience of Chicana and Chicano scholars. *Qualitative Studies in Education, 11*(1), 121–136.

Solórzano, D. G., Villalpando, O., & Oseguera, L. (2005). Educational inequities and Latina/o undergraduate students in the United States: A critical race theory analysis of their educational progress. *Journal of Hispanic Higher Education, 4*(3), 272–294.

Stage, F. K. (2007). Answering critical questions using quantitative data. In F. K. Stage (Ed.), *New Directions for Institutional Research: No. 133. Using quantitative data to answer critical questions* (pp. 5–16). San Francisco, CA: Jossey-Bass.

Stage, F. K., & Wells, R. S. (2014). Critical quantitative inquiry in context. In F. K. Stage & R. S. Wells (Eds.), *New Directions in Institutional Research: No. 158. New scholarship in critical quantitative research—Part 1: Studying institutions and people in context* (pp. 1–7). San Francisco, CA: Jossey-Bass.

Teranishi, R. T. (2007). Race, ethnicity, and higher education policy: The use of critical quantitative research. In F. K. Stage (Ed.), *New Directions for Institutional Research: No. 133. Using quantitative date to answer critical questions* (pp. 37–49). San Francisco, CA: Jossey-Bass.

EBELIA HERNÁNDEZ is an assistant professor in the Department of Educational Psychology at Rutgers, The State University of New Jersey.

NEW DIRECTIONS FOR INSTITUTIONAL RESEARCH • DOI: 10.1002/ir

7

This chapter discusses the evolution of the critical quantitative paradigm with an emphasis on extending this approach to new populations and new methods. Along with this extension of critical quantitative work, however, come continued challenges and tensions for researchers. This chapter recaps and responds to each chapter in the volume, and concludes the two-volume series with a look toward the future use of quantitative criticalism by institutional researchers and higher education scholars.

Past, Present, and Future of Critical Quantitative Research in Higher Education

Ryan S. Wells, Frances K. Stage

This volume of *New Directions for Institutional Research* (*NDIR*) is the third to address the topic of critical quantitative inquiry in the past eight years. Stage (2007) introduced the concept to institutional researchers and higher education scholars, with a variety of chapters from respected researchers of higher education. Following publication, there was noticeable interest in this approach to inquiry among researchers, scholars, and graduate students. Continued interest was evident from a 2012 symposium at the Association for the Study of Higher Education (ASHE), which was full of engaged participants and which generated thoughtful and interesting discussions (Carter et al., 2012). That event prompted us to revisit and update the critical quantitative concept in print. We garnered enough interested authors and readers, and were encouraged by supportive editors, to produce two volumes on critical quantitative inquiry, confirming that it remained a salient concept for higher education research.

In *New Scholarship in Critical Quantitative Research—Part 1* (Stage & Wells, 2014), we extended the original two aims of critical quantitative work to include a third. As updated, critical quantitative work aims to:

- use data to represent educational processes and outcomes on a large scale to reveal inequities and to identify social or institutional perpetuation of systematic inequalities in such processes and outcomes;
- question the models, measures, and analytic practices of quantitative research in order to offer competing models, measures, and analytic

NEW DIRECTIONS FOR INSTITUTIONAL RESEARCH, no. 163 © 2015 Wiley Periodicals, Inc.
Published online in Wiley Online Library (wileyonlinelibrary.com) • DOI: 10.1002/ir.20089

practices that better describe the experiences of those who have not been adequately represented; and

- conduct culturally relevant research by studying institutions and people in context.

Building on the work in the two previous *NDIR* volumes, the theme for this volume is "new populations, new approaches, and new challenges." In the higher education community, the idea of critical quantitative inquiry is now past the introductory stage and is experiencing some maturity. It is precisely at this time that quantitative and critical scholars should reflect not only on if and how quantitative criticalism has been useful in the past, but how the concepts can be extended to be even more useful in the future. Part of this reflection should include an examination of the limitations, tensions, and potential drawbacks of using this paradigm in new ways. This entire volume was meant to serve these purposes, and we conclude by recapping and responding to the preceding chapters as we look to the future of quantitative criticalism.

New Populations

Past work explicitly employing a critical quantitative framework has examined issues related to gender (Kinzie, 2007; Williams, 2014), immigrant status (Conway, 2014; Wells, 2010), and low-income students (Oseguera & Hwang, 2014). The majority of research employing the critical quantitative approach, however, has focused on issues of race and ethnicity (e.g., Alcantar, 2014; John & Stage, 2014; Perna, 2007; Teranishi, 2007; Williams, 2014). Despite this emphasis, there are still racial and ethnic subgroups that have been neglected not only in higher education literature but also in the conversations about critical quantitative research. This exclusion is especially important because these often overlooked and marginalized groups are precisely those that can and should be examined through a critical quantitative lens.

In Chapter 1, Faircloth, Alcantar, and Stage address the need for a more critical approach to the analysis of large-scale data sets when studying the educational conditions and subsequent academic outcomes for American Indian and Alaska Native students. A limitation not easily addressed includes the problem of representing the differences in two very different groups of peoples—American Indians and Alaska Natives (AI/AN)—who typically are grouped for purposes of analyses. Another challenge is the diversity represented by persons from more than 600 federally and state recognized tribes who speak more than 200 different Indigenous languages. Other constraints include sampling problems, faulty identification of AI/AN respondents through reliance on self-reports, and nonresponse problems for particular survey items.

New Directions for Institutional Research • DOI: 10.1002/ir

The authors also discuss the limitations of analyses using models developed decades ago based on normative college student experiences. They describe drawbacks in relying on typical variables and suggest alternative approaches that could be more relevant to the experiences of AI/AN students. Finally, the authors suggest analysis techniques that are useful for identifying critical variables when analyzing data with small samples.

In Chapter 2, Vaccaro, Kimball, Wells, and Ostiguy address another marginalized and often overlooked group of students in institutional research and higher education literature: students with disabilities. They detail the challenges and opportunities for studying students with disabilities and discuss the importance of asking research questions that are considered in relation to institutional, legal, and equity issues. They provide analysis and discussion of typical measures used for the study of students with disabilities, and make their own suggestions for considering ways of grouping students with disabilities for analysis purposes. This discussion of obstacles and suggestions for overcoming them highlights the ways a critical approach can not only enrich the scholarly literature but also inform faculty and staff so that institutions ultimately may better serve college students.

The first two chapters bring new populations into the critical quantitative discussion, but this is only the tip of the iceberg for populations that researchers appear to feel are either unnecessary to study or too difficult to do so, given the challenges of data collection and analysis. However, suggestions and themes from these chapters can be applied to many more subpopulations of students. English-language learners (ELLs) often are overlooked, for example, but are likely have unique challenges related to particular first languages and pathways that warrant critical inquiry (e.g., Fernández, 2002; Maloney, 2003). Although immigrant students have been examined to some degree, the range of immigrant experiences, as well as refugee experiences, deserves more attention. Religious minorities are also often marginalized on college campuses where Christian privilege dominates (Seifert, 2007) and deserve a critical examination of their experiences, pathways, and outcomes in college.

Additionally, while Oseguera and Hwang (2014) illuminated pathways for low-income students, the broad issue of social class has received less attention than warranted, especially by critical researchers. This is a particularly promising avenue, given that the foundation of critical quantitative inquiry originates with critical theory, such as that which grew out of the Frankfurt School, with a focus on revealing inequality, changing society, and emancipating the oppressed. Critical quantitative inquiry could serve as an orientation to a renewed study of class inequality in higher education. A focus on social class is also timely as social inequality is, for the moment at least, back in the public and political discourses.

New Approaches

In addition to extensions of critical quantitative inquiry to a number of new populations, it can also be a useful paradigm when coupled with other research designs and methods. Rios-Aguilar begins that conversation in Chapter 3 by discussing the much-talked-about phenomenon of big data. As with so many innovations, technical developments, or new analytic tools, big data can be used in a number of ways. Rios-Aguilar demonstrates why use of big data without a critical orientation may, at best, limit what can be discovered about the experiences of students in higher education or, at worst, continue to propagate inequities or marginalizing tendencies. The depersonalizing and disempowering aspects of data mining in order to understand students can easily propagate majority narratives while silencing the minority.

However, Rios-Aguilar demonstrates the power big data can have when harnessed through a critical lens. This perspective is likely to grow in importance as big data become more and more prevalent and as institutional researchers are encouraged to use these data along with predictive analytics and other techniques to, it is hoped, understand the full range of student experiences. Finally, Rios-Aguilar suggests a deliberate and focused effort on the part of institutional researchers and scholars to use big data in a targeted manner that helps us learn more about what works to promote success for underrepresented students. Michael Funk (2012) refers to this kind of scholarship on underrepresented students as a strength-based approach.

In Chapter 4, Malcom-Piqueux introduces another set of techniques—person-centered approaches—that can help those aiming to conduct quantitative studies from a critical perspective. She explains how the subtle shift from variable-centered approaches to these strategies, including latent class analysis and related methods, can reveal more nuance than traditional approaches. Importantly, she does this through an example related to college financing strategies. This topic is in dire need of new critically oriented approaches, given the disparate impacts of increasing tuitions and debt loads for students of color and low-income students, for example (Ginsberg, 2011; Greenstone & Looney, 2013). More broadly, person-centered techniques have promise for studying any of the populations discussed earlier in relation to their college experiences.

As researchers think about the college experience, it has been well documented that peers, social connections, social capital, and relationships are important for success. And as critical researchers are well aware, these factors are likely to be even more essential for underserved and underrepresented students (Hurtado, Alvarez, Guillermo-Wann, Cuellar, & Arellano, 2012). However, the most recent analytic tools have yet to be brought to bear critically on these aspects of higher education. In Chapter 5, González Canché and Rios-Aguilar inform us of ways to close this gap by using critical social network analysis (CSNA). They not only present a concrete example of how to use social network analysis in higher education but also demonstrate how it can be used in a critical manner to explore and reveal inequities, leading to recommendations for change in policies and structures.

Importantly, their chapter (along with Rios-Aguilar in Chapter 3) addresses the needs of community college students. Despite the fact that 45% of college students matriculate at community colleges and most of the underrepresented groups we have discussed in the volume are overrepresented in those institutions (American Association of Community Colleges, 2014), even critical scholars tend to disproportionately focus on four-year institutions. As we extend our critical inquiry to new methods and approaches, studying "institutions and people in context" must include a greater number of studies examining less selective institutions of higher education, and particularly community colleges.

While these new approaches are exciting, and the chapters herein demonstrate the potential power they have to help change institutions and society to better serve marginalized students, there are many more possibilities. For example, the critical *qualitative* community often achieves some of its critical aims by employing participatory methods. There is no reason that critical *quantitative* researchers cannot also use techniques such as participatory survey research and related approaches (e.g., Bensimon & Malcom, 2012; Maddocks, Novkovic, & Smith, 2011: Parrado, McQuiston, & Flippen, 2005). Involving the populations of students we hope to serve better not only helps us to address more relevant research questions in an appropriate manner but also has the potential to immediately impact students and empower them as student-researchers.

Quantitative techniques that are often thought to be so grounded in positivism as to be diametrically opposed to critical approaches should also be reconsidered. While not all quantitative researchers will agree—given the ongoing critique of critical quantitative from the positivist quantitative community (Stage & Wells, 2014)—we propose that both experimental and quasi-experimental critical designs be pursued. For example, a regression discontinuity design utilizes a threshold, or cut point, where some individuals receive the "treatment" and others do not. While acknowledging the problematic notion of a top-down "treatment" that is provided to some students and not others, there still may be ways to leverage the approach for critical ends. If an intervention were purposefully designed such that a pretest or measurement of the salient construct was utilized to create the threshold for a programmatic or policy intervention, those most in need of the service would be precisely those who receive it. Using regression discontinuity in this way could not only provide researchers with a causal estimate for the most relevant populations but may also enable researchers to use the results to provide opportunities to positively impact those students' experiences immediately.

New Directions for Institutional Research • DOI: 10.1002/ir

Additionally, researchers who focus on underrepresented students often have difficulty with missing variables. Oseguera and Hwang (2014) used the Educational Longitudinal Study (ELS) to study college access for low-income students using a critical quantitative approach. Their theory reflected experiences of the low-income population as well as other relevant variables. Because the sample size was already low, they used multiple imputation techniques to impute values. By using the imputation technique, they were able to reduce loss of cases through missing data, allowing for more robust analysis of already small populations.

Are those extended approaches adequately critical? Do they somehow taint the aims of either the quantitative approach or the critical approach by attempting to join them? These are precisely the types of questions that must be rigorously and purposefully addressed if critical quantitative inquiry is to continue to develop in the future.

New Challenges

That daunting task of wrestling with conceptual and practical questions related to critical quantitative inquiry is highlighted by Hernández in Chapter 6. She worked on a critical quantitative project with various team members bringing different strengths, backgrounds, experiences, and assumptions about both quantitative and critical research. Her chapter is especially helpful in thinking about the very real and important tensions inherent in this work. Her notion that a critical approach "challenges normative assumptions and research practices in 'quantitative research'" (p. 95) is insightful. As shown in Chapter 1 for Native American students and in Chapter 2 for students with disabilities, very practical considerations of sample size can provide roadblocks to research and therefore limit the generation of new knowledge. Vaccaro and coauthors offer some suggestions to continue to study students with disabilities in spite of such issues, but the necessarily limited suggestions challenge normative assumptions about "significance" in educational research.

Even more fundamentally, Hernández points out that what various researchers mean by "critical" may not be the same and may prove very difficult to reconcile. In a 2009 article titled "Learning From Our Differences," Moss and coauthors, representing widely differing views about appropriate methods in educational research, attempted to discuss frankly the apparent divide between quantitative and qualitative researchers. In doing so, they invoked Kuhn's (1962) concept of incommensurable paradigms. The classic example that they utilized involves the concept of "mass" from physics. We all learn what mass is at some point in our K–12 education from a Newtonian perspective, only to learn at some later point that, from an Einsteinian perspective, mass means something quite different. How are we to use the term "mass" in a useful and meaningful way, when it means two very different things, things that are similar in certain ways, and which are both quite useful?

The term "critical" seems similar at times. What this term may mean to various researchers depends on their worldview, socialization to research, and educational background, each of which may differ. This is true even in the qualitative realm, with Frankfurt-style critical theory, critical race theory (CRT), LatCrit, queer theory, and others all having some commonality but differing in important ways as well. The differences only grow when combining the term "critical" with the term "quantitative" and attempting to answer just what it means for each individual or project.

One step in this direction, as Chapter 6 suggests, is to communicate in print precisely what the author means by "critical," how that term informs the work, and how that perspective influences the findings. This is in line with recommendations from others (e.g., Rios-Aguilar, 2014) for all researchers, not only qualitative researchers, to include a positionality statement in their writing. In the past, when quantitative methods were used, the assumption was that postpositivist or positivist epistemology underpinned the research; this may no longer be adequate.

As we complicate such notions, transparency of perspective is a key component of the conversation. While we expect that editors and reviewers of quantitative articles may push back on such practices, that tension is precisely the place where opportunity exists for meaningful dialogue and debate. The challenge for some institutional researchers to be transparent in this way may prove even more daunting as campus administrations and leaders may not see the need for, or may frankly disagree with, a critical perspective and approach. Again, however, if a critical perspective in quantitative research is to advance, it is precisely these small proactive efforts that might move the needle on higher education research. Such subtle attempts at conversation in print should then complement those difficult and important in-person conversations, good examples of which Hernández and her colleagues have provided.

Pamela Moss, one of the contributors to the conversation in the article "Learning From Our Differences," stated, "a key touchstone of high-quality social science for me is openness and responsiveness to challenge from alternative perspectives, where we each make an ethical commitment to understand alternatives in their strongest possible light, to risk our own prejudgments, and to search for differences as well as commonalities among the alternatives" (Moss et al., 2009, p. 514). To us, this seems like a good place from which to start as we encourage deeper and more meaningful dialogue around the uses for, and limitations of, a critical quantitative approach to research. The article goes on to say: "We can each hold our own perspectives and learn from the challenges others raise, even when we disagree" (p. 514).

NEW DIRECTIONS FOR INSTITUTIONAL RESEARCH • DOI: 10.1002/ir

Conclusion

We conclude this two-volume series by thanking the chapter authors who braved uncharted territory. They stepped forward to explore new techniques; to describe their experiences in reconciling their research techniques, strategies, and values alongside other researchers; and to uncover new experiences about underrepresented and marginalized populations. We challenge institutional and higher education researchers to join these authors in simultaneously expanding, enriching, and critiquing this work as you develop your own formulations of quantitative inquiry that broaden perspectives, uncover inequity, and generate new ways of thinking about the broad array of populations participating in and served by higher education.

References

Alcantar, C. M. (2014). Civic engagement measures for Latina/o college students. In F. K. Stage & R. S. Wells (Eds.), *New Directions for Institutional Research: No. 158. New scholarship in critical quantitative research—Part 1: Studying institutions and people in context* (pp. 23–36). San Francisco, CA: Jossey-Bass.

American Association of Community Colleges. (2014). *2014 fact sheet.* Washington, DC: Author. Retrieved from http://www.aacc.nche.edu/AboutCC/Documents/FactS heet_2014.pdf

Bensimon, E. M., & Malcom, L. (Eds.). (2012). *Confronting equity issues on campus: Implementing the equity scorecard in theory and practice.* Herndon, VA: Stylus Publishing.

Carter, D. F., Kuntz, A., Gildersleeve, R. E., Mayhew, M., Stage, F., & Wells, R. (2012, November). *Critical quantitative inquiry: The grounding, use, critiques, and future of a methodological paradigm.* Symposium presented at the Association for the Study of Higher Education annual meeting, Las Vegas, NV.

Conway, K. M. (2014). Critical quantitative study of immigrant students. In F. K. Stage & R. S. Wells (Eds.), *New Directions for Institutional Research: No. 158. New scholarship in critical quantitative research—Part 1: Studying institutions and people in context* (pp. 51–64). San Francisco, CA: Jossey-Bass.

Fernández, L. (2002). Telling stories about school: Using critical race and Latino critical theories to document Latina/Latino education and resistance. *Qualitative Inquiry, 8*(1), 45–65.

Funk, M. S. (2012). *Making something of it: The untold stories of promising Black males at a predominately White institution of higher education* (Unpublished doctoral dissertation). University of Massachusetts Amherst.

Ginsberg, B. (2011). Administrators ate my tuition. *Washington Monthly.* Retrieved from http://www.washingtonmonthly.com/magazine/septemberoctober_2011/features/adm inistrators_ate_my_tuition031641.php?page=all

Greenstone, M., & Looney, A. (2013, July). *Rising student debt burdens: Factors behind the phenomenon.* Washington, DC: The Hamilton Project.

Hurtado, S., Alvarez, C. L., Guillermo-Wann, C., Cuellar, M., & Arellano, L. (2012). A model for diverse learning environments. In J. C. Smart & M. B. Paulsen (Eds.), *Higher education: Handbook of theory and research* (Vol. 27, pp. 41–122). New York, NY: Springer.

John, G., & Stage, F. K. (2014). Minority serving institutions and the education of U.S. underrepresented students. In F. K. Stage & R. S. Wells (Eds.), *New Directions for Institutional Research: No. 158. New scholarship in critical quantitative research—Part 1: Studying institutions and people in context* (pp. 65–76). San Francisco, CA: Jossey-Bass.

Kinzie, J. (2007). Women's paths in science: A critical feminist analysis. In F. K. Stage (Ed.), *New Directions for Institutional Research: No. 133. Using quantitative data to answer critical questions* (pp. 81–93). San Francisco, CA: Jossey-Bass.

Kuhn, T. S. (1962). *The structure of scientific revolutions* (2nd ed.). Chicago, IL: University of Chicago Press.

Maddocks, J., Novkovic, S., & Smith, S. M. (2011). Measuring performance for accountability of a small social economy organization: The case of an independent school. *Canadian Journal of Nonprofit and Social Economy Research, 2*(1), 45–60.

Maloney, W. H. (2003). Connecting the texts of their lives to academic literacy: Creating success for at-risk first-year college students. *Journal of Adolescent & Adult Literacy, 46,* 664–673.

Moss, P. A., Phillips, D. C., Erickson, F. D., Floden, R. E., Lather, P. A., & Schneider, B. L. (2009). Learning from our differences: A dialogue across perspectives on quality in education research. *Educational Researcher, 38*(7), 501–517.

Oseguera, L., & Hwang, J. (2014). Using large data sets to study college education trajectories. In F. K. Stage & R. S. Wells (Eds.), *New Directions for Institutional Research: No. 158. New scholarship in critical quantitative research—Part 1: Studying institutions and people in context* (pp. 37–50). San Francisco, CA: Jossey-Bass.

Parrado, E. A., McQuiston, C., & Flippen, C. A. (2005). Participatory survey research integrating community collaboration and quantitative methods for the study of gender and HIV risks among Hispanic migrants. *Sociological Methods & Research, 34*(2), 204–239.

Perna, L. W. (2007). The sources of racial-ethnic group differences in college enrollment: A critical examination. In F. K. Stage (Ed.), *New Directions for Institutional Research: No. 133. Using quantitative data to answer critical questions* (pp. 51–66). San Francisco, CA: Jossey-Bass.

Rios-Aguilar, C. (2014). The changing context of critical quantitative inquiry. In F. K. Stage & R. S. Wells (Eds.), *New Directions for Institutional Research: No. 158. New scholarship in critical quantitative research—Part 1: Studying institutions and people in context* (pp. 95–108). San Francisco, CA: Jossey-Bass.

Seifert, T. (2007). Understanding Christian privilege: Managing the tensions of spiritual plurality. *About Campus, 12*(2), 10–17. doi:10.1002/abc.206

Stage, F. K. (Ed.). (2007). *New Directions for Institutional Research: No. 133. Using quantitative data to answer critical questions.* San Francisco, CA: Jossey-Bass.

Stage, F. K., & Wells, R. S. (Eds.). (2014). *New Directions for Institutional Research: No. 158. New scholarship in critical quantitative research—Part 1: Studying institutions and people in context.* San Francisco, CA: Jossey-Bass.

Teranishi, R. T. (2007). Race, ethnicity, and higher education policy: The use of critical quantitative research. In F. K. Stage (Ed.), *New Directions for Institutional Research: No. 133. Using quantitative data to answer critical questions* (pp. 37–49). San Francisco, CA: Jossey-Bass.

Wells, R. S. (2010). Children of immigrants and educational expectations: The roles of school composition. *Teachers College Record, 112*(6), 1679–1704.

Williams, K. L. (2014). Strains, strengths, and intervention outcomes: A critical examination of intervention efficacy for underrepresented groups. In F. K. Stage & R. S. Wells (Eds.), *New Directions for Institutional Research: No. 158. New scholarship in critical quantitative research—Part 1: Studying institutions and people in context* (pp. 9–22). San Francisco, CA: Jossey-Bass.

RYAN S. WELLS *is an associate professor of higher education in the Department of Educational Policy, Research, and Administration at the University of Massachusetts Amherst.*

FRANCES K. STAGE *is a professor of higher and postsecondary education in the Department of Administration, Leadership, and Technology at New York University.*

NEW DIRECTIONS FOR INSTITUTIONAL RESEARCH • DOI: 10.1002/ir

INDEX

Abberley, P., 28
Adams, D. W., 19
AERA. *See* American Educational Research Association (AERA)
AHEAD. *See* Association on Higher Education and Disability (AHEAD)
AI/AN students. *See* American Indian or Alaska Native (AI/AN) students
Alcantar, C. M., 5, 12–14, 24, 97, 104
Allatta, J., 79
Alon, S., 64
Alvarez, C. L., 106
American Educational Research Association (AERA), 98
American Indian or Alaska Native (AI/AN) students: critical analysis of, 8–9; critical theory of change, 19–20; implications for policy and research, 17–18; issues associated with studies of, 14–17; large-scale national education data sets for, 9–13; PK–12 national data sets, 9–12; postsecondary data sets for, 12–13; recommendations for future research, 18–19; state of education for, 7–8
Andersen, E. B., 65
Andresen, E. M., 28
Antonio, A., 75
Arellano, L., 106
ASHE. *See* Association for the Study of Higher Education (ASHE)
Association for the Study of Higher Education (ASHE), 103
Association on Higher Education and Disability (AHEAD), 37
Astin, A., 75
Aud, S., 9, 14–16, 64

Baez, B., 72
Barker, A., 44
Barron, K. E., 61
Bearinger, L. H., 7
Beginning Postsecondary Study (BPS), 12–13
Bender, F., 29

Bensimon, E. M., 107
Berger, J. B., 36
Bettinger, E., 48
Beyond the Asterisk: Understanding Native Students in Higher Education, 16
Biancani, S., 76, 77
Big data, 43–55; benefits of, 45–49; challenges of, 49–52; and critical quantitative research in higher education, 55; and critical thinking, 50–51; definitions of, 44–45; in higher education research, 52–55; interpretation of, 49–50; as meaningful data, 50; and new data classes, 51–52; overview, 43; real-time data and, 46–47; and scholarly activity, 49
Blackorby, J., 35
Blair, J. J., 29
Board Of Governors Grant (BOGG), 86
BOGG. *See* Board Of Governors Grant (BOGG)
Boyd, D., 44, 49–51
Brayboy, B. M. J., 9, 18
Breiger, R. L., 79
Brinckerhoff, L. C., 30
Brockelman, K. F., 34
Brooks-Gunn, J., 7
Bryman, A., 28
Burr, S., 46

Cabrera, A. F., 61
Cahalan, M., 12
Calderone, S., 63
Caldwell, J. Y., 5
Calizona Community College (CCC), 81
Carducci, R., 98
Carrington, P., 78
Carsey, A. C., 29
Carter, D. F., 75, 103
Castagno, A. E., 9, 18
CCC. *See* Calizona Community College (CCC)

113

NEW DIRECTIONS FOR INSTITUTIONAL RESEARCH
ORDER FORM SUBSCRIPTION AND SINGLE ISSUES

DISCOUNTED BACK ISSUES:

Use this form to receive 20% off all back issues of *New Directions for Institutional Research*.
All single issues priced at **$23.20** (normally $29.00)

TITLE	ISSUE NO.	ISBN
_____	_____	_____
_____	_____	_____
_____	_____	_____

Call 1-800-835-6770 or see mailing instructions below. When calling, mention the promotional code JBNND to receive your discount. For a complete list of issues, please visit www.josseybass.com/go/ndir

SUBSCRIPTIONS: (1 YEAR, 4 ISSUES)

☐ New Order   ☐ Renewal

U.S.	☐ Individual: $89	☐ Institutional: $341
CANADA/MEXICO	☐ Individual: $89	☐ Institutional: $381
ALL OTHERS	☐ Individual: $113	☐ Institutional: $415

Call 1-800-835-6770 or see mailing and pricing instructions below.
Online subscriptions are available at www.onlinelibrary.wiley.com

ORDER TOTALS:

Issue / Subscription Amount: $ _____

Shipping Amount: $ _____
(for single issues only – subscription prices include shipping)

Total Amount: $ _____

SHIPPING CHARGES:

First Item	$6.00
Each Add'l Item	$2.00

(No sales tax for U.S. subscriptions. Canadian residents, add GST for subscription orders. Individual rate subscriptions must be paid by personal check or credit card. Individual rate subscriptions may not be resold as library copies.)

BILLING & SHIPPING INFORMATION:

☐ **PAYMENT ENCLOSED:** *(U.S. check or money order only. All payments must be in U.S. dollars.)*

☐ **CREDIT CARD:** ☐ VISA ☐ MC ☐ AMEX

Card number _____ Exp. Date_____

Card Holder Name_____ Card Issue # _____

Signature _____ Day Phone _____

☐ **BILL ME:** *(U.S. institutional orders only. Purchase order required.)*

Purchase order # _____
Federal Tax ID 13559302 • GST 89102-8052

Name_____

Address_____

Phone_____ E-mail_____

Copy or detach page and send to: **John Wiley & Sons, One Montgomery Street, Suite 1000, San Francisco, CA 94104-4594**

Order Form can also be faxed to: **888-481-2665**

PROMO JBNND

Great Resources for Higher Education Professionals

College Athletics and the Law

12 issues for $225 (print) / $180 (e)

Develop a legally sound "game plan" for your institution's athletic programs! Each month, you get expert coaching on how to meet NCAA and Title IX requirements, negotiate coaching contracts, support athletes with disabilities, and more.

collegeathleticslaw.com

FERPA Answer Book and Bulletin

6 issues for $220 (print only)

Includes a full binder with all you need to know about FERPA

From safekeeping students' education records to learning how you can share personal information, this is your professional survival guide. It includes the latest changes to the regs, how to comply, and newly issued FPCO policy letters, administrative and judicial decisions, and more.

About Campus

6 issues for $65 (print only)

An exciting and eclectic mix of articles — designed to illuminate the critical issues faced by both student affairs and academic affairs as they work on their shared goal: to help students learn. Topics include promoting student learning, meeting the needs of a diverse student population, assessing student learning, and accommodating the changing student culture.

Assessment Update

6 issues for $135 (print) / $110 (e)

Get the latest assessment techniques for higher education. *Assessment Update* is your resource for evaluating learning communities, performance indicators, assessing student engagement, using electronic portfolios, new assessment approaches and more.

assessmentupdate.com

Recruiting & Retaining Adult Learners

12 issues for $225 (print) / $180 (e)

This publication addresses the challenges and opportunities you face in recruiting, retaining, and educating your adult students. Find strategies to target your orientation to adult learners, encourage adult-friendly support systems, take advantage of new technologies, and more.

recruitingretainingadultlearners.com

The Successful Registrar

12 issues for $230 (print) / $185 (e)

Get practical guidance on all aspects of your job—from implementing the newest technology and successful registration programs to complying with FERPA, and from training your staff and student workers to security issues and transcript management.

thesuccessfulregistrar.com

The Department Chair

4 issues for $99 (print) / $89 (e)

From retaining your best faculty and resolving conflict to measuring learning and implementing new policies, this resource arms you with the practical information you need to manage your department effectively.

departmentchairs.org/journal.aspx